# Real Men Pray

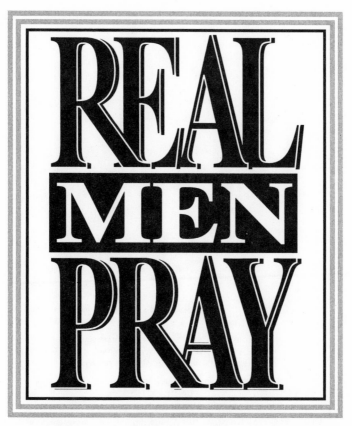

# PRAYER THOUGHTS FOR HUSBANDS & FATHERS

Thomas Couser

SAINT LOUIS

The weekly activity pages were developed and written by Kenneth Wagener and Dawn Mirly Weinstock.

Copyright © 1996 Concordia Publishing House
3558 S. Jefferson Avenue, St. Louis, MO 63118-3968
Manufactured in the United States of America

1 2 3 4 5 6 7 8 9 10     05 04 03 02 01 00 99 98 97 96

To Peter, Mark, and Katie

# CONTENTS

........................................

## P R E F A C E

I must admit that, for most of my life, prayer was more a source of frustration than comfort. I have many gifts, but a long attention span is not one of them. Having been instructed in my early years to "close your eyes and bow your head when you pray," I often found my mind wandering. Ten seconds into my meditation and my thoughts turned to my next appointment or an upcoming golf game. How could I be a faithful disciple when I couldn't even prepare properly for the battle?

That all changed when I started to keep a prayer journal. I enjoy writing. It was natural to sit down and express my prayer thoughts with pen in hand. Not all my prayer thoughts are here. Some are so personal I only share them with God. But I think you'll get the idea.

These prayers are divided into 52 weeks, roughly following the calendar year. After each trio of prayers, you'll find a page to guide your own prayer thoughts. Buy a notebook, and as you read through the prayers, Bible references, inspirational quotes, and reflection questions, jot notes for your own prayer life. Include a list of people (don't forget yourself), important events (birthdays, meetings, church activities), and spiritual issues that you need to bring before God in prayer. Your journal may include notes or "formal" prayers. Either way, you will find it helps you focus your thoughts on a heartfelt talk with your heavenly Father.

I have many duties in this life. I might be a teacher to those who sit in my Bible class, a counselor to those in the youth group at my church, or a coach to those on my basketball team, but to three people, I am the most important male in their life. I am their father. What an awesome responsibility. I can teach parenting classes, but when I open the door at home, I step into a reality that I feel ill-prepared to face.

Many of these prayers center on life at home. They focus on my challenges and responsibilities as a father and husband. The serious business of fathering carries added responsibility in a Christian household. By God's grace and the leading of His Holy Spirit, I must not only pass on the heritage of faith but model discipleship. I hope through sharing these prayers, you will be strengthened in your commitment to share your faith with those around you, whether with your wife, children, friends, or business associates.

I don't confess to have all the answers. These prayers point out how vulnerable I am. They are a start toward a better understanding of myself and the task God has put before me. I hope they serve the same purpose for you. Our conversations with God are a vital part of our daily walk with Him.

God has some awesome plans in store for us as Christian men. May God bless you on the path He has set before you.

Thomas Couser

# W E E K 1

Where do you dive into a book this big? Try the beginning. In the beginning God and Adam walked and talked together—one-on-one. When sin separated man and God, direct conversation ceased, except for rare occasions when God appeared to His people. But God promises to hear us—when we pray. And He promises to answer us. So begin at your comfort level and tell God what's in your heart.

..............................................

# Open Doors

Lord, Your continued providence astounds me.
You impact my life in ways that I could
    never imagine.
Now You are providing me with a
    new opportunity.

Lord, I ask Your continued presence as I move
    into the future.
May I see each day not as a completed journey
    but as a single step on the path
    You have set for me.
Help me wait with patient anticipation to
    see what other surprises await.
Guide me as I step forward,
    trusting Your promise to be with me always.

I consecrate this day to You.
I ask that You bless it and my future as
    only You can.
Be a part of my tomorrow, just as You were
    my yesterday.

Father, thank You for the daily blessings
    You shower on my life. Amen.

# Stepping Out in Faith

*When Joseph woke up, he did what the angel of the Lord had commanded him and took Mary home as his wife. (Matthew 1:24)*

What an example of trust You have given us
    in Your servant Joseph, Lord.
He was in love yet so intent on
    doing the right thing.
But his desire to do what was morally right
    was surpassed by his desire
    to serve You.

When Your angel spoke to Joseph, he listened.
He believed the angel's words, and
    he acted.
Joseph trusted Your Word that Mary's child
    was special, was conceived by the Holy Spirit.
He didn't demand proof, he stepped out in faith
    and took Mary into his home.

Father, we all benefited from Joseph's actions.
    Mary gained a loving spouse.
    Jesus had a loving earthly father.
And the Savior of all was born—and Joseph
    gave Him the name Jesus.
Help me learn from Joseph, Lord.
Open my ears so that I may hear
    Your plan for me.
Guide my actions so my wife, children,
    and those around me may see and feel
    Your presence in my life. Amen.

# Spiritual Boldness

As I read from Acts today, Father,
I was amazed by the spiritual boldness
   Peter and John displayed
   as they shared the Gospel.
Threats couldn't stop them.
Seeing their brothers and sisters in the faith
   suffering, even giving their lives,
   didn't deter them.
In all situations, they shared Jesus' love.

Such Christian boldness isn't common today.
I certainly don't see it in myself.
   I'm easily intimidated, often afraid.
I avoid doing what God expects of me.
   I end up feeling guilty.

Father, open my eyes to see Jesus as the
   solution for my sins—including the
   sin of spiritual timidity.
Remind me of the boldness of His action,
   His willingness to die for others.
Move me to celebrate daily the
   new life He won for me.
Through the power of Your Holy Spirit,
   make me a bold disciple of Your Son. Amen.

# Week 1 Activities

**Themes:** Beginnings, courage, expectation, faith, future, journey, obedience

**Old Testament Exploration:** Genesis 12:1–7; Joshua 1:1–9

**New Testament Exploration:** Acts 4:1–31; 2 Corinthians 4:7–18

> Faith is to believe, on the Word of God, what we do not see, and its reward is to see and enjoy what we believe.
>
> *St. Augustine*

> Fear knocked at the door. Faith answered. No one was there.
>
> *Anon.*

> To have faith is to believe the task ahead of us is never as great as the Power behind us.
>
> *Anon.*

## Reflect

How does the idea of life as a journey apply to you today? Whose courage has most inspired you? Why? What are the milestones ahead in your journey with Christ? Think about a time when God helped you through a personal hardship. How did God strengthen you? How did God use the experience to bring you closer to Him and deepen your trust in Him? Ask God to prepare you for the journey ahead.

# W E E K  2

Do your actions reflect the faith God has given you? Even your youngest child measures your words against your actions. God has chosen you. What an awesome thought, but one that carries tremendous responsibility. He has appointed you to be His witness to your family, to friends, and even to strangers. Ask God to guide your words and actions that they may demonstrate your faith in Him.

..........................................

..........................................

# I've Hurt Their Feelings

Forgiving Father, I knew the moment I said it,
    I was wrong.
But once words are out, you can't
    take them back.

Now they won't talk to me.
I'm responsible for the wall between us.
I love them, but my "I'm sorry" just doesn't
    seem to be enough right now.

Lord, You know all about forgiveness; You're
    the Champion Forgiver.
Touch their lives right now, just as
    You are touching mine.
Break through the wall with Your love and
    help us restore the relationship.

Provide me with a full measure of Your wisdom.
Enable me to say the right things
    now and in the future.
May the love of Christ be evident in
    our relationship again. Amen.

# The Church Service

Here I am—*again!*
The pastor drones on and on, and my mind
    slips farther and farther away.
The kids fidget, and I wonder if it's
    worth it.

I tried to start with the right attitude.
    We sang a soul-stirring opening hymn.
But I took Mark to the bathroom during
    the Scripture reading, and I couldn't get
    tuned in when we came back.

I really enjoy our church's fellowship.
But I don't feel like I'm being
    spiritually fed.
I'm not challenged in my discipleship.
I've heard that from others too.
    "Pastor's sermons lack content."
    "He needs to be more dynamic in his delivery."

But he preaches God's Word, and his
    messages are doctrinally sound.
Am I the problem?
Perhaps I'm not preparing properly.
    I'm letting form get in the way of content.

Lord, help me get the most out of the
    worship service.
May it prepare me for my ministry
    in Your world. Amen.

........................................

# A Chance Meeting

Father, thanks for the opportunities You give
  to share my faith.
It happened again today when
  You opened the door.
She told me she was
  living with her boyfriend. She asked
  what I did for a living.
My response embarrassed her.
I apologized and told her that even
  if I didn't agree, I could still listen.
She said I was more understanding than
   her parents.
I told her that as a dad
  I could empathize with their concerns.
  We laughed at that.

She spoke of her religious upbringing.
  Guilt was separating her from God.
"Talk to God about your situation,"
  I suggested. "Ask for His forgiveness and
  His guidance. He will forgive you
  for Jesus' sake."

Then I advised her to discuss marriage.
  "It might do wonders for your relationship
  with your parents and with God."
She said she would, and I believed her.

Thanks, Father, for that opportunity to
  share Your love and forgiveness.
Thanks, too, for guiding me to the
  right words. Amen.

...............................................

# Week 2 Activities

**Themes:** Forgiveness, gentleness in speech, reconciliation, regret, renewal, witness, worship

**Old Testament Exploration:** Isaiah 43:1–13; Jeremiah 1:4–19

**New Testament Exploration:** 2 Thessalonians 2:13–3:5; 1 Peter 3:8–16; 1 John 1:9

> Jesus ... wants us to see that the neighbor next door or the people sitting next to us on a plane or in a classroom are not interruptions to our schedule. They are there by divine appointment. Jesus wants us to see their needs, their loneliness, their longings, and he wants to give us the courage to reach out to them.
>
> *Rebecca Manley Pippert*

> Our task is to live our personal communion with Christ with such intensity as to make it contagious.
>
> *Paul Tournier*

> Humanity is never so beautiful as when praying for forgiveness, or else forgiving another.
>
> *Jean Paul Richter*

## Reflect

Think about your Christian witness in the past weeks. List some examples of how God has used you to spread the Good News. Were there any times you avoided sharing your faith, whether through actual words or through actions? How is forgiveness a part of your witness to your family and friends? How will God's Holy Spirit strengthen you in your personal witness? Pray that God would guide your words and actions that they may be a light on the hill.

........................................................

# WEEK 3

Fear stalks us. Satan whispers, "God can't protect you from violence, bigotry, or disappointment. After all, He couldn't protect His Son from the cross." But God says, "Have no fear." He points you to the cross Satan ridicules. God reminds you Jesus went willingly to His death—to complete God's salvation plan. The empty grave assures you that with God, you have nothing to fear.

........................................

# Guarding Their Welfare

*[Herod] was furious, and he gave orders to kill all the boys in Bethlehem and its vicinity who were two years old and under. (Matthew 2:16)*

Jesus, my children walk in danger every day.
We live in a violent society. Guns and drugs are
    a way of life for many children.
Can You identify with that?
    I think You can.
You faced the threat of an angry king,
    a man who resorted to murder to
    protect his throne.
But Your heavenly Father intervened.
He told Joseph, your earthly protector,
    to take You and Mary and flee to Egypt.
    And You were spared.

Grant me the wisdom and courage to
    listen to Your guidance as I raise my family.
Send Your Spirit to guide me as I strive to
    guard my children from the
    evils of this world.
Cause my actions to be directed by love,
    not an angry reaction to things I
    can't control.

Jesus, Your earthly father, Joseph,
    set the example. He trusted God, and
    God provided the way out.

Once again Joseph stepped out in faith,
   trusted the angel's words, and
   through his actions You, my Savior,
   were delivered from danger.
Help me develop that same trust in
   my heavenly Father's guidance as
   I strive to ensure
   my children's future. Amen.

......................................

# Martin Luther King Jr. Day

Father, we pause today to consider a time
    when hatred and bigotry ruled our land;
A time when all people didn't have the same
    opportunities and privileges;
A time when obvious divisions based on
    the color of one's skin existed.

I suspect You are more than a
    little disappointed that we had to overcome
    such a problem in the first place.
But such divisions arise from our sinfulness.
They expose our distance from
    You and Your idea of perfection.

Father, in love You sent Your Son to
    save the *whole* world.
Jesus' suffering, death, and resurrection were
    for *all* people, regardless of
    race, color, or creed.
In Jesus, You unite all who believe into
    one family—brothers and sisters of Jesus,
    working together in Your kingdom.
Such unity might be difficult for the world
    to understand, but make it a
    reality in my life.
Through the power of Your Spirit,
    help me overcome my hidden prejudices and
    accept all people as
    Your precious children.
Help me seek ways to serve those
    You place in my path. Amen.

........................................

# Disappointment

I'm having a tough time, Lord.
Things have happened that seem unfair.
More than just being a victim of
    circumstance,
        people I trusted have let me down.
I'm not only depressed, I'm
        having trouble trusting—
        and it's affecting all my relationships.

Lord, help me overcome this
        disappointment.
You can provide the emotional healing I need.
Renew me with Your Holy Spirit.
Remind me that I can always
        trust You.
Your promises of love and constant support are
        more than certain.
Despite earthly setbacks,
        my eternal life in Your loving presence
        is assured.
May that Good News sustain me. Amen.

............................................

# Week 3 Activities

**Themes:** Anxiety, disappointment, prejudice, protection, trust, unity

**Old Testament Exploration:** Psalm 56; Ecclesiastes 1:1–11; 9:1–12

**New Testament Exploration:** Romans 5:1–11; 2 Corinthians 1:3–11, 18–22; Philippians 3:1–11

> But when [a man] feels himself doubting, let him practice faith, fight against doubt, and labor to recapture certainty, in order that he can say: I know that I am accepted by God and have the Holy Spirit, not for the sake of worthiness or merit on my part, but for the sake of Christ. ...
>
> *Martin Luther*

> Out of every disappointment there is treasure. Satan whispers, "All is lost." God says, "Much can be gained."
>
> *Frances J. Roberts*

## Reflect

What do you fear right now? How is the devil working in your life to rattle the foundation of your faith? How is God working to bring you closer to Him? Because Jesus said, "Come to Me, all you who are weary and burdened," how do you respond? How does Jesus' promise to help carry your burdens make you feel? Ask God to strengthen your trust in Him.

# WEEK 4

Whom do you work for? Is it a company? a person? yourself? Do you work for personal satisfaction or identity? for the paycheck? Any answer is only partially correct for the Christian. You have a higher calling, a heavenly employer. Ask God to show you His direction for your life. As He reminds you that you really do everything for Him, your earthly job will take on new meaning.

...........................................

........................................

# Knowing My Role

*[John said,] "But after me will come one who is more powerful than I, whose sandals I am not fit to carry."* (*Matthew 3:11*)

It's a struggle to keep things
    in perspective right now, Lord.
I've experienced some success.
Praise, and even adoration, is coming my way.
I'm not used to this. But … I like it.

So here I am, feeling a little guilty.
All the credit should go to You.
I am what I am through the Holy Spirit's power.
    But I like the attention.
How do I control my ego and keep my
    role in perspective?

John the Baptist was the ultimate point man.
    He knew his role was to prepare the way and
    point people to You—their Savior.
Through Your Spirit, make me willing to
    give You all the glory and praise
    my actions invite.
Forgive me for the times I accept the accolades
    meant for You. Amen.

# Affluence

An affluent culture surrounds me.
My neighbors' lifestyles beckon me.
I often want material things to
   "keep up with the Joneses."

I know I shouldn't covet, but
   fancy cars, expensive clothes, and
   the hedonistic lifestyle entice me.
Even my children expect the right clothes,
   the latest music and videotapes,
   the trendiest gadgets.
But it's all superficial; real wealth
   isn't measured by worldly standards.
My greatest treasure can't be seen—
   Jesus' saving love.

Lord, give me strength to resist coveting
   what others have.
Grant me wisdom to make good choices.
May my lifestyle, my words, and thoughts
   reflect who I am—Your forgiven child.
Help me pass these values on to
   those I love. Amen.

# My Job

Thanks for my job.
I don't always say that, Lord, but today
   it's on my mind.
I heard Ted is out of work again, and
   Jim told me he's concerned about
   cutbacks at the plant.
I'm grateful for a steady income.
Where would our family be without it?
Thanks, too, for my health so
   I can work.

But I struggle with the "sameness" of my job
It takes patience to do the same thing with
   the same people every day.
And some people get to me.
   There's Hal, who's always complaining, and
   Mary, who's never on time.
And my boss—he has no concept of what
   it's like in the trenches.

Lord, help me endure these things.
Help me see my job as "my ministry."
Keep me aware that You put me in
   this job as part of Your plan.
Show me the opportunities I have to
   minister to those around me.
May I always look for ways to
   share Your love
   with others through my job. Amen.

# Week 4 Activities

**Themes:** Contentment, humility, success, treasure, wealth, work

**Old Testament Exploration:** 2 Samuel 7:1–17; Ecclesiastes 5:18–20

**New Testament Exploration:** Acts 20:13–38; Ephesians 5:1–20

> Work is not primarily a thing one does to live, but the thing one lives to do. It is, or should be, the full expression of the worker's faculties, the thing in which he finds spiritual, mental, and bodily satisfaction, and the medium in which he offers himself to God.
>
> *Dorothy L. Sayers*

> Let us work as if success depended upon ourselves alone; but with heartfelt conviction that we are doing nothing and God everything.
>
> *St. Ignatius of Loyola*

> Work, work, from early until late. In fact, I have so much to do that I shall spend the first three hours in prayer.
>
> *Martin Luther*

## Reflect

List three good things about your job. List three people with whom you enjoy working. How has God blessed your work? What opportunities does He give you in your work to serve Him? How has God challenged you to improve yourself and others at work? List three work-related items to pray about during the next week.

# W E E K  5

Problems on the job. Problems at home. No
money. No time off. You're about to explode.
Retreat! Take your Bible and find a quiet spot.
Read your favorite passage or look up Psalm 46.
Talk to God about what's going on in your life.
He cares. He wants to help. Listen for His answer.
Take a deep breath and walk back into the world,
assured of God's strengthening presence.

................................................

# A Job Interview

It started as a casual lunch with a friend.
Then there was a follow-up phone call.
Now I'm getting ready for an interview.

Lord, I didn't plan on this.
I'm basically happy with my job.
There are things I'd like to change,
    but I appreciate the security.
But a new position would mean new
    challenges and opportunities.
That's exciting … and terrifying.

Father, through all this help me
    seek Your will.
You have given me talents and abilities
    and even potential I haven't realized yet.
Lord, keep me open to change.
Give me the insight to make the
    the right decisions.
Fill me with the security that comes from
    following Your plan.
Service to You and to Your kingdom are
    what I most desire.
Through Your Spirit, enable that to happen.
    Amen.

# Values

*[Jesus'] disciples came to Him, and He began to teach them. (Matthew 5:1–2)*

Jesus, there's a clash between
    the values You taught in the
    Beatitudes and those of today's world.
You used words like *meek* and *poor* and
    *merciful*.
To be honest, those aren't
    fashionable words anymore.

The results of the Beatitudes are great.
All Christians long for
    heaven.
But I don't want to take a path that includes
    persecution and suffering.

I'm looking for a middle road.
I want You to say, "Strive for these things,
    but I understand your situation."
But You didn't say that.
Instead You told us to
    rejoice and be glad in suffering.
That's crystal clear.
You have high expectations for
    Your disciples.
You paid a high price to ensure
    that our failures won't condemn us.
And You sent the Holy Spirit to work faith
    in me and set me
    on the high road to heaven.

Because of Your actions, I want to
   change my lifestyle to meet Your standards,
   not the world's.

Thanks for paying the price.
Please send Your Holy Spirit to empower me to
   follow You. Amen.

........................................

# Stress

Pressure.
It's building inside me.
   Deadlines to meet.
   Demands to fulfill.
I'm struggling to stay afloat.
But it's my family that's really suffering.
   They see less of me, and when I am around,
   I'm tired and irritable.

Stress.
It's even driving a wedge
   between You and me, Lord.
I've let everything else in my life
   take priority over
   time spent with You.

That's the key.
When I try to handle everything myself,
   remind me to turn to You, Lord.
Help me submit to Your will instead of
   struggling to make my own path.
Forgive my attempts to go it alone.
Strengthen my trust in You and Your plan.
   Amen.

# Week 5 Activities

**Themes:** Change, lifestyle, stress, talents, values

**Old Testament Exploration:** Exodus 3:1–4:17

**New Testament Exploration:** Romans 12:1–21;
1 Corinthians 12:1–11

> Talent is God-given; be thankful. Conceit is self-given; be careful.
>
> *Thomas La Mance*

> Beatitudes, just by virtue of having been spoken by him, have enriched our mortal existence beyond imagining, putting a yeast of love into the unlively dough of human greed and human spite and human willfulness, so that it can rise marvellously.
>
> *Malcolm Muggeridge*

## Reflect

What are the major decisions before you today? How can you use your talents to serve Christ in your work? In your faith walk, do you take the path of least resistance? Ask God to strengthen you for the walk He has set before you. List your major sources of stress (poor job situation, lack of time for kids or wife, dirty garage). How does God help you overcome the stress of home and work? Take steps to eliminate at least one cause of stress this week. Thank God for the ability to take control in this area.

......................................................

# W E E K  6

Love in Christ abides forever,
Fainting not when ills attend;
Love, forgiving and forgiven,
Shall endure until life's end.

# Childbirth

There she is Lord; I can't believe
   it's a girl.
I stand here watching in awe as You perform
   another miracle in my life.
I don't deserve these blessings, but now
   You have given me a daughter
   to go with my two sons.
I look at my wife, lying there peacefully now.
   Lord, bless her recovery.
She is a part of me. She enriches my life
   immeasurably.

Now, a girl … I don't know how to act.
   I know baseballs and fire trucks best.
I don't dare bring them into her nursery.
   Dolls and lace seem more appropriate.
She's so tiny now. I wonder whom she'll
   grow up to look like.
I have an idea—her mother.

Lord, bless our growing family.
Keep us anchored in Your love that we might
   be one, just as Your Son makes us
   one with You. Amen.

# Valentine's Day

It's Valentine's Day and here I am
   again, standing in the middle of the
   greeting card section, looking for the cards
   with the right sentiments.
Why do I always wait till the last minute?
Every year I promise to plan ahead, and
   every year my life gets more complicated.
Then one day I look at the calendar and
   it's February 14th!

Lord, I know the importance of
   communicating my love.
Through Word and Sacrament,
   You constantly remind me of
   Your love and forgiveness.
Help me daily
   celebrate the love
You have placed in my life—
   for my wife,
   my children,
   my family,
   my friends,
   and for You. Amen.

..........................................

# The Ultimate Motive

*Jesus replied, " 'Love the Lord your God. … Love your neighbor as yourself.' " (Matthew 22:37, 39)*

What a simple four-letter word, *love*,
   with multiple meanings.
Perhaps an overused word:
   "I *love* that picture."
   "I would *love* to do that with you."
   "I *love* you."

Love requires commitment.
Jesus' commands imply we have no option.
Love is to be the
   root of all actions.
We must constantly ask, "Is this the
   *loving* thing to do?"

*Love,* as a verb, means action.
*Love,* as the basis for all
   I do and say,
   becomes the driving force in my life.
My mission statement is a statement of
   love.

Jesus, forgive my lack of love and compassion.
As I look to the cross, move me to see
   Your suffering and dying as an act of love.
May that sacrificial act and Your Spirit
   work within me a
   life of service in Your name.
Jesus, that's the real meaning of love. Amen.

# Week 6 Activities

**Themes:** Childbirth, children, commitment, family, fatherhood, love, marriage

**Old Testament Exploration:** Genesis 1:27–28; Isaiah 63:7–9

**New Testament Exploration:** 1 Corinthians 13; Philippians 4:10–19

> Kids are not a short-term loan, they are a long-term investment!
>
> *Anon.*

> The greatest benefits God has conferred on human life, fatherhood, motherhood, childhood, home, become the greatest curse if Jesus Christ is not the head.
>
> *Oswald Chambers*

> Becoming a father is easy enough, but being one can be rough.
>
> *Wilhelm Busch*

> Christian love links love of God and love of neighbor in a twofold Great Commandment from which neither element can be dropped, so sin against neighbor through lack of human love is sin against God.
>
> *Georgia Harkness*

## Reflect

What are the challenges before me today as a husband? as a father? What might I learn about love from my family? What areas do I need to ask God to help me in as a father and husband? Ask God to increase the love in your life and help you share it with others.

# W E E K   7

"The Cardinals win the pennant! The Cardinals win the pennant!" The emotion in announcer Jack Buck's voice was unmistakable—JOY! Sports victories often cause a mad exuberance in us. Shouldn't God's gift of faith, His presence in your life, cause the same feeling? Whether you're eating, shooting hoops, or sitting quietly at your Lord's feet, ask Him to fill you with holy joy.

..................................................

..........................................

# Breakfast

Perhaps because I'm a
    morning person,
I enjoy breakfast more than
    any other meal.
The smell of fresh coffee, the crunch of toast,
    and the warm feeling as oatmeal
    settles into my stomach—
I love breakfast time.

I scan the sports section for the
    latest scores.
The kids wander down to join me before
    heading off to school.
It's a time to check in and wish them
    Godspeed before we head in
    different directions.

Breakfast prepares us for the day.
It's not just proper nourishment for the body,
    it's proper preparation for the mind.
Breakfast is being in touch with each other and
    being in touch with You, Lord.

So pull up a chair and join us, Lord.
Listen in on our conversations and
    renew us with Your Spirit for the day ahead.
I want You to be part of my life and the
    lives of those I love.

We're all here together now.
What a glorious beginning to
    a glorious day. Amen.

## Personal Victory

It would be so easy to gloat, Lord.
What started as a little difference of opinion
    escalated into a major disagreement.
Through it all I stood my ground,
    not so much because I felt I was right but
    because I believed it was Your desire.
The facts were presented today, and it was
    there for all to see.
I wanted to say, "I told you so."

I'm grateful I didn't seize the moment
    to boast.
I would have taken the glory away from You.
    You got me through the tough times.
    I found my strength in You.
Thank You—not because I look good
    but because Your will is being done.

Lord, help me build on this success.
May others see me in a new light.
May they see Your love dwelling in me.
You have put me in this position for a
    specific purpose.
Make that purpose clear to me. Amen.

........................................

# Sports

Competition has become our
    driving force.
Success has become our goal.
If you don't believe me, look at
    the playing field. If we no longer
    actively play a sport, we live out
    our fantasies through our children.

Sports strengthen the body and mind.
But don't they sometimes destroy the spirit?
How about when success becomes all-important?
    When victory must come no matter the cost?
What are we teaching our children—
    our values or God's values?

Paul talks about training for and
    running the race.
But it's not an earthly competition.
This race ends in a heavenly reward.
    But it's a race we can't win—no matter
    how hard we try or how much
    we want the prize.
Only Jesus has completed the race, and
    He left a well-marked course for
    us to follow.
And as members of His family,
    Jesus runs beside us, sometimes even
    carrying us, until we reach the prize—
    eternal life.

Thanks, Lord, for a competition truly
    worth winning. Amen.

............................................

# Week 7 Activities

**Themes:** Competition, leisure, pleasure, relaxation, success

**Old Testament Exploration:** Genesis 39:20–23; 2 Kings 18:5–7

**New Testament Exploration:** 1 Corinthians 9:24–27

> Success is neither fame, wealth, nor power; rather it is seeking, knowing, loving, and obeying God. If you seek, you will know; if you know, you will love; if you love, you will obey.
>
> *Charles H. Malik*

> Where your pleasure is, there is your treasure: where your treasure, there your heart; where your heart, there your happiness.
>
> *St. Augustine*

## Reflect

What priority do you place on success? What priority do you place on leisure? What priority do you place on relationships? What priority do you place on quiet time with your Lord? Ask God to help you place the proper emphasis on work, play, and worship this week.

# WEEK 8

You've heard the axiom "count to 10" before you lash out at someone. It's amazing what God can do in 10 seconds. He can calm your temper, slow your heart rate, and unclench your fists. He helps you walk away or at least gain a more rational outlook. Imagine if you counted to 20 or took a walk around the block! Ask God to help you work on being a peacemaker.

..........................................

# Family Fights

Everyone seems to be mad at everybody else
  right now.
Father, I know that every family goes through
  times like these.
But that doesn't make me feel better, and it
  definitely doesn't make it easier.

I ask Your forgiveness for my part in
  our dispute.
I've been on edge lately.
Things aren't the best at work, and I'm
  bringing some of those feelings home.
But I can't change other peoples' attitudes.
And don't I need to have my needs met too?

Where will all this end unless someone
  acts soon?
We love each other, but the anger of the
  moment will take us down a path
  we don't want to follow.
Father, things must change, and I guess
  it needs to start with me.

Grant me the wisdom and strength I need to
  be Your leader in our home right now.
Help me to be a peacemaker
  rather than a provoker.
May the love of Jesus that Your Spirit planted
  inside me come to the surface.
Bring peace to our home, and let it
  begin with me. Amen.

# Evenings at Home

It's been a while since I spent
  an evening like this.
Katie reminded me.
Thanks for her message, Lord.

So tonight I stayed home.
We played games, talked, and giggled.
I fixed their cocoa before bedtime and
  listened to their prayers.
It might not seem like much, but it's
  precious to me.

The time we have together is so short.
Peter is away now; can Mark and Katie
  be far behind?
The days of youth are numbered.
Soon they won't want to play Uno with Dad or
  ask to be tucked in bed.
Lord, I don't want to look back and
  think about what I missed.

Slow me down. Help me plan more
  nights like this.
Katie reminded me that she needs them,
  but I need them too.
Now as I sit here catching up on my reading,
  You call me in Your Word.
That's right, I'm Your child.
Let's spend some time together. Amen.

# A Walk in the Woods

Thank You, Father, for life's little wonders.
While attending a meeting out of town,
    I decided to get some exercise.
But the hotel didn't have an exercise room.
I asked at the front desk, and
    the clerk directed me to a park
    down the street.
I never found the park, but I did find a path.
    What a joy!

The path wound through a wooded area and
    came out
    next to a stream.
I followed the stream to a river.
Then I found myself on a bluff.
    I could see the whole countryside.
I sat and meditated on Your
    magnificent creation.
I started out for some exercise and
    ended up with a spiritual experience.

Lord, thanks for special times with You.
Thanks for giving me the trust to walk
    an unknown path.
You constantly surprise me and teach me
    through Your beautiful world. Amen.

................................

# Week 8 Activities

**Themes:** Communication, creation, disagreements, peace, relationships, spirituality, togetherness

**Old Testament Exploration:** Genesis 1:9–13; 33:1–20; Psalm 29

**New Testament Exploration:** Hebrews 13:1–8; 1 Thessalonians 4:1–18

> In life troubles will come which seem as if they never will pass away. The night and storm look as if they would last forever; but the calm and the morning cannot be stayed; the storm in its very nature is transient. The effort of nature, as that of the human heart, ever is to return to its repose, for God is peace.
>
> *George Macdonald*

> First keep the peace within yourself, then you can also bring peace to others.
>
> *Thomas à Kempis*

> Any deep relationship to another human being requires watchfulness and nourishment; otherwise, it is taken from us. And we cannot recapture it. This is a form of having and not having that is the root of innumerable tragedies.
>
> *Paul Johannes Oskar Tillich*

## Reflect

How have I been a peacemaker in my relationships at home and work? What strengths has God
given me through my family and friends? Have I
thanked God for them? List your favorite "home"
activities. When was the last time you did any of these
things? Schedule at least one this week. When was the
last time you read your Bible? prayed? took a walk and
talked with God? After dinner, take a walk through
your neighborhood and praise God for all that's good
in your life.

We never read about Jesus making travel plans. In fact, He counseled His disciples not to worry about the future. Jesus knew His travels would end at the cross, but it didn't concern Him. He trusted His Father's plan. And God has a plan for you too. The path He lays before you, and along which He guides you, leads to heaven. What a glorious future!

........................................

# The Death of a Friend

The news came suddenly.
The words cut into my heart, and I was
    consumed with grief.
Nothing prepares you for news like that.

Father, I sit here quietly, waiting for
    the service to begin.
His lifeless body, encased in a wooden box,
    sits before me.
As I view the casket, I'm overwhelmed by
    memories of times together.
I cherish them, longing for more.

Father, I don't question Your intervention.
    Only You know the plan predestined for us.
But I'm grateful that You
    merged our lives together
    for a time.
You were part of that friendship.
The joy and hope You brought to
    that earthly fellowship sustains
    me now.

In You there is always a future.
Father, in the midst of my sorrow,
    enable me to celebrate eternal life.
Help me put aside my feelings and
    glorify You for his new life with You.
May my words and actions bear testimony to
    the faith You have given me. Amen.

# The Future

Lord, I know it's wrong, but I'm
   worried and concerned
   about the future.
Most of my anxiety involves personal issues.
   Where am I going?
   What will I be doing?
   What about my health and the welfare of
   my family?
There are so many unknowns, so many
   challenges.
Do I have the strength and energy to
   face them?

As I contemplate these issues, I realize
   it's a selfish agenda.
I want to protect my future,
   my status,
   my turf.
To do so, I make decisions that
   will bring me to my desired outcome.
I want to control my future.

But the future, like the past,
   belongs to You, Lord.
Worrying doesn't alter Your plan.
I should be concerned with how
   my goals match up with
   Your desires for my life.
I need to learn to depend on You
   for guidance instead of worrying
   how I will determine my future.

Then I will be living my life to Your glory.

Help me move ahead, confident that
    my future, as well as my family's,
    is in Your hands.
Assure me of Your love and
    forgiveness. Amen.

..........................................

# Worry

*But seek first His kingdom and His righteousness, and*
*all these things will be given to you as well. (Matthew*
*6:33)*

The words are right there, "Do not worry about
   your life …"
Jesus, You've convicted me again.
   Worry is part of my life.
I worry about my health, the family budget,
   whether the car will last till it's
   paid for, and countless other things.
I worry about survival.

As I continue reading, I reach the section where
   You discuss our heavenly Father's
   understanding of our needs.
You were drawing on personal experience,
   weren't You?
Your Father provided all the
   spiritual, emotional, and physical support
   You needed.
You went to Him in prayer and
   relied on His Word to fight Satan.

"Give me some of that trust, God, and I
   promise not to worry," I respond.
Then I realize, God already has answered
   my prayer.
   He's given me You, Jesus.

All my worries are about earthly things.
But You, Jesus, have taken care of the

important spiritual things.
Your victory on the cross and over the grave
    ensures eternal life.
You defeated sin, the ultimate worry.

Lord, help me put aside my worries
    about trivial things.
Help me concentrate on the Good News of
    salvation.
May others see the peace and contentment
    You give to me. Amen.

# Week 9 Activities

**Themes:** Anxiety, comfort, death, future, guidance, life, trust, worry

**Old Testament Exploration:** 1 Kings 19:9–21; Psalm 23

**New Testament Exploration:** Romans 8:28–39; Philippians 4:4–9

> Do not look forward to what may happen tomorrow; the same everlasting Father, who cares for you today, will take care of you tomorrow, and every day. Either he will shield you from suffering or he will give you unfailing strength to bear it.
>
> *St. Francis de Sales*

> Lord Jesus, make my heart sit down.
>
> *African proverb*

> I look upon life as a gift from God. I did nothing to earn it. Now that the time is coming to give it back, I have no right to complain.
>
> *Joyce Cary*

## Reflect

What do you see in your future? How might your desires and expectations differ from God's plans for your future? What would you like your friends and family to say about you at your funeral? Ask God to help you live your life in such a way to make these statements true. Why don't you need to fear the future—even death? Thank God for His Son, your Savior, and for His guiding hand.

# WEEK 10

Mountains figure prominently in the action recorded in God's Word. Life-changing events such as the near-sacrifice of Isaac, the giving of the Ten Commandments, Jesus' transfiguration, and His ascension occurred on mountains. David used the apparent permanence of mountains as a metaphor for God's strength. Thank God for such magnificent reminders of His power.

..................................................

..........................................

# Mountains

Inspiring beauty overwhelms me,
    even from a distance.
Actually being in the mountains awakens
    an awesome respect for Your majesty, Lord.
Your entire creation reflects Your glory.

I love being in the mountains:
    fresh, clean air,
    brilliant blue skies,
    mind-clearing heights that give me
    a new perspective.
I feel closer to You, Father, in the mountains.
Looking toward a distant peak, it's as if
    my future rolls out before me.
Your activity in my life becomes
    apparent—past, present, and future.

But I can't stay in the mountains.
As I leave, I pray that this visit
    will prepare me for my time on the
    plains and even the valleys of life.
Lord, come with me, wherever the road leads.
Thanks for the mountains and this
    intimate visit with You. Amen.

# Transformed

*Jesus took with Him Peter, James and John the broth-er of James, and led them up a high mountain by themselves. There He was transfigured before them. (Matthew 17:1–2)*

Jesus, I don't understand what happened on
    that mountaintop.
I know it was something glorious.
    Your face shone like the sun.
    The Old Testament prophets joined You
    in a divine conversation.
    Everyone was enveloped in a cloud.
It was a glorious moment, an affirmation of
    who You are and what You are about.
And the voice contributed Your Father's
    seal of approval:
    "This is My Son. Listen to Him."

How were the lives of those
    present transformed that day?
My initial reaction is ... very little.
    James and John argued over who was
        number one.
    Peter got caught in an act of denial.
But then I note the immediate results.
    They saw You in Your glory.
And they followed that image until it led
    to a cross and Your ultimate sacrifice.

That's it for me.
There are so many glorious
    experiences in my life.

It's a matter of seeing You in them.
Through the power of Your Spirit,
    remind me that because of Your death
    and resurrection, every day has the
    potential to be a transforming
    experience.
Help me live as Your forgiven child. Amen.

# Your Word

"Your word is a lamp to my feet and a
      light for my path."
I've recited those words many times.
I've spoken them in worship and even
      shared them with friends during
      times of struggle.
But today, Lord, the message came to me.

As You know, I've been struggling, Father.
Friends have tried to help, but it seemed that
      even my appeals to You were unanswered.
And then, while preparing for a Bible class,
      Your Spirit guided me to the right words.
The message was loud and clear—it was
      exactly what I needed to hear.

The spiritual battle isn't over, but Your Word
      gave me the direction I needed.
I've found comfort in the knowledge that
      You are with me and forgive my
      shortcomings.
Father, thanks for rescuing me and
      setting me back on course.
And thanks for the gift of
      Your powerful Word. Amen.

# Week 10 Activities

**Themes:** Affirmation, change, discipleship, glory, grandeur, inspiration, transformation, the Word

**Old Testament Exploration:** Isaiah 6:1–7

**New Testament Exploration:** Matthew 17:1–9; 2 Corinthians 3:7–18

> You're a man, you've seen the world—
> The beauty and the wonder and the power,
> The shape of things, their colors, lights,
>     and shades,
> Changes, surprises—and God made it all!
>
> *Robert Browning*

> Many follow Jesus to the breaking of bread, but few to the drinking of the cup. Many reverence his miracles, few follow the ignominy of his cross. Many love Jesus so long as no adversities befall them, many praise and bless him so long as they receive any consolations from him; but if Jesus hides himself and leaves them but a little while, they fall either into complaining or into too much dejection of mind.
>
> *Thomas à Kempis*

> Other books were given for our information, the Bible was given for our transformation.
>
> *Anon.*

## Reflect

What mountaintop experiences has God given to you? How has the Lord been with you in the valleys? What transformations do you see God working in your life right now? Ask God this week to guide you as you read and share the Word of eternal life.

........................................................

# WEEK 11

Remember when your mom would offer you a
chocolate from her Valentine's gift? You'd grab
what looked like something nutty, but it was
inevitably a raspberry chew. Yuck! Then you
wised up and nibbled the corner first to test it.
God recommends the same approach in your
faith life: "Test everything. Hold on to the good."
He will lead you to those things that will
strengthen your faith.

........................................

...........................................

# A Repentant Attitude

*But later he changed his mind and went. (Matthew 21:29)*

Repentance or hypocrisy?
Jesus, there is little doubt which one
    I would willingly choose.
Your message of Good News calls me to
    repentance time and time again.
My failure to respond not only causes me pain,
    but it affects those I love.
But like King David, I long for Your forgiveness,
    and I return to You.

There are times when I'm a hypocrite as well,
Occasions when I break promises to You and to
    those I work with, to those I love.
And so it is that I find identity with both
    characters in the parable of the two sons.
I'm a living contradiction.

Jesus, save me from these inconsistencies.
Make my life one of willing service to You.
May those around me see me as more than
    friend, co-worker, husband, father
But as a model of discipleship, hearing
    Your commands and responding.
In those times when I fail, bring
    me back to You and to Your
    ever-present love.
May the Gospel be a consistent influence
    in my life. Amen.

# Temptation

*Then the devil left Him, and angels came and attend-
ed Him. (Matthew 4:11)*

Jesus, Your personal battle with Satan
    provides a powerful lesson.
You met him in the desert, one on one, and
    came away the victor.
You depended on the Word of Your Father
    to deliver You.

I want to be like You, totally
    dependent on God for victory.
I fall victim to temptation when I trust my own
    strength to outlast the devil's trickery.
I lose all the battles that I don't let God
    fight for me.

Jesus, You won that battle against Satan, but
    it was just one of many.
In fact, You were still fighting the battle
    when You went to the cross.
Being truly human, You must have been
    tempted to use Your Godly powers.
You must have been tempted to tell
    Your accusers and persecutors
    what You really thought of them.
But You won that battle too.
You went like a sheep to the slaughter.
You took all our sins on Yourself,
    all the times we succumb to the
    Tempter's power,

and You suffered, and died,
and rose again.
You won for us the final victory over Satan.

Such servanthood in action amazes me.
I stand in awe of Your conviction,
Your power.
Then I realize that You have promised to be
with me in my battles with Satan.
Your Spirit will focus me on the Word
and Your cross.

May Your will be done in my life. Amen.

# Avoiding Those Who Might Lead Astray

*Test everything. Hold on to the good. Avoid every kind of evil.* (*1 Thessalonians 5:21–22*)

What a confusing world we live in.
With so many conflicting messages,
   it's hard to figure out
   right from wrong.
And if I'm aware of the messages,
   my children must see and hear them too.

Even within the family of believers,
   people try to lead us astray.
They twist Your Word, take it out of context.
Even those who claim faith might not have the
   good of Your kingdom in mind.
Without realizing, we can be diverted from
   the path of salvation.
You warn us to test the messages
   against Your Word.
Keep the good; avoid the bad.

Then You remind me that
   any path that doesn't
   lead to Jesus is the
   wrong path.
Keep this truth before me.
   Help me pass it along to my children.
Guide my actions that they
   may reflect Your love and
   Your presence in my heart. Amen.

# Week 11 Activities

**Themes:** Hypocrisy, repentance, service, sorrow, temptation

**Old Testament Exploration:** Genesis 3:1–24; Numbers 21:4–9

**New Testament Exploration:** Matthew 4:1–11; 21:28–31; John 6:68

> [God] will incline us to repent, but he cannot do our repenting for us.
>
> *A. W. Tozer*

> Temptation is God's magnifying glass; it shows us how much work he has left to do in our lives.
>
> *Erwin W. Lutzer*

> Temptation provokes me to look upward to God.
>
> *John Bunyan*

## Reflect

What temptations are you facing in your life today? How does God's promise in 1 Corinthians 10:13 help you when you are tempted? List the times you know you've succumbed to the devil's temptation. Write a prayer of confession. Read the prayer out loud. Then read 1 John 1:9 and Ephesians 1:3–8. Throw the paper away as you thank God for His forgiveness.

# WEEK 12

Hours spent commuting. Time spent in airports. Lonely nights spent in hotel rooms. Work requires a lot of time. But you can spend some of it with God. Listen to praise tapes or a Christian radio station in the car. Bring a Christian book for the wait at the airport. Pack a Bible and a study guide for the next road trip. Make traveling for work a vacation with God.

..........................................

........................................

# Business Trips

Travel goes with my job, Lord.
But I don't enjoy it anymore.
Some people envy those who travel.
It might look glamorous,
    but hotel rooms and restaurant food
    soon grow old.
I long for the affection of my family,
    the comfort of my own bed, and a
    home-cooked meal.

But You have placed me in this job.
I might be hundreds of miles away from home,
    but You're with me.
The surroundings might change, but
    Your loving presence is constant.
Help me live in that joy.
May my faith shine even though I'm
    tired and lonely.
Through the power of Your Spirit, enable me to
    be Your witness.
And as I look forward to a joyous reunion
    with my family, remind me that
    an even more joyous eternal celebration
    awaits me. Amen.

# On Coming Home

Father, it's so good to be home.
I've only been gone one night, but I missed
   this place.
I got excited just pulling in the driveway.
It's good to be here, but things happened while
   I was away.
While most were trivial, some events were
   very important
   like the A+ or the fish that died.
My enthusiasm for what
   happened in my life might not be shared by
   all.
Someone might even resent my absence.

I remember a story You told about a
   young man who returned home
   after a disastrous trip.
We usually focus on his shame
   and repentance and his father's forgiveness
   and acceptance.
But there were other feelings.
   Someone was angry and hurt.
Lord, make me sensitive to others so
   my homecoming might be a
   celebration for everyone. Amen.

# A Day Off

Lord, the coffee tastes perfect
    this morning.
Perhaps it's because I have time to
    enjoy it.
I'm glad I decided to take
    the day off.
I've got chores to do but nothing pressing.

Father, I really needed this day.
The intensity of my daily pressures
    was taking its toll.
I just had to take a time-out.
So if I need this day, why do I feel so guilty?
Why do I have to force myself to relax?
Lord, is something wrong with
    my lifestyle?

Father, there's a lesson here.
You set a pattern when You rested on
    the seventh day.
You made it a special day, the Sabbath.
It was so important that You
    made it one of Your Commandments.

Father, give me the fortitude to change
    my lifestyle.
Slow me down and help me experience
    times like this often.
Father, during these days of rest,
    help me find renewal in You.
Lord, only in You can I find real rest. Amen.

..........................................

# Week 12 Activities

**Themes:** Absence, business, family, rest, reunion, travel

**Old Testament Exploration:** Genesis 2:2–3; Deuteronomy 31:1–8

**New Testament Exploration:** Luke 15:11–31; 2 Timothy 1:3–7, 13–14

> Work can be used as a defensive shield. There are men who bring work home every evening so as to have an excuse for not entering into any serious conversation with their wives or children. Others barricade themselves behind the newspaper as soon as they get home, pretending to be deeply absorbed in it when their wives try to tell them of their troubles.
>
> *Paul Tournier*

> Contentment is not the fulfillment of what you want, but the realization of how much you already have.
>
> *Anon.*

> Take rest; a field that has rested gives a bountiful crop.
>
> *Ovid*

## Reflect

List the last three vacations or days off you took. What did you do? Did you spend as much effort taking time off as you do at work? When you come home from work or a business trip, do you throw up a "defensive shield"? Ask God to help you spend time with your wife and children. Thank God for the many gifts He's given you—a job, a family, friends, faith, and …

# W E E K  1 3

Mentors advise, act as sounding boards, even prepare you for your life's work. A good mentor
doesn't make a decision for you, but through discussion, he guides your deliberations. God provides something better than mentoring. Through
time spent in His Word, through time spent at
His Table, He talks with you and prepares you
and gives you *His grace* to do your job as His servant.

.......................................................

# Wind

It blew in suddenly.
I became aware of the sound
    as I watched TV.
I'd heard warnings, but this was serious.
A glance out the door reinforced my concern.
Trees swayed and anything not secured
    seemed in motion.
The for-sale sign in my neighbor's yard
    disappeared into the night.
I feared for my life and for
    my family's safety.

The wind subsided during the night.
There's some damage, trees down and an
    awning ripped from its frame.
My neighbor's sign found a
    new home down the street,
    embedded in a hedge.
Small caucuses gathered around the
    neighborhood to survey the damage and
    talk about our luck.
Lord, You provided a lesson in that storm.
I was really afraid.
    Your protecting hand held me.
It's the same during life's storms.
My world may seem in turmoil, but
    You are still in charge.
I can rest secure in You.
Help me share that comfort with
    those I love. Amen.

.........................................

# Mentors

*To Timothy my true son in the faith.* (*1 Timothy 1:2*)

So few words but what a
   tremendous message.
The first lines of Paul's first letter to Timothy
   provide such insight.
Paul knew who he was;
The resurrected Christ had confronted him
   personally.
Paul responded to Jesus' loving command
   and shared his Savior's love with
   everyone he met.
He also lovingly befriended Timothy, a
   "true son" in the faith.
The guidance Paul must have provided—
   the influence he must have had on
   Timothy.

Thank You, Lord, for the Pauls in my life.
My parents, pastors, teachers,
   co-workers, and mature Christians who
   took time to share.
What an impact they've had.
As I listened and watched them live the faith,
   I came to understand the realities of
   discipleship.

Lord, I doubt my abilities to
   be a mentor to someone else.
I have flaws and shortcomings.

My family and friends must see them,
    especially when I'm under pressure.
Still, You want me to
    model discipleship for others.
To some young person, I am Paul.
Lord, through the power of Your Holy Spirit,
    empower me for that noble task. Amen.

# Music

I awoke to the sound this morning.
It was my companion as I drove to the office.
It plays softly as I work.
My world is full of music.

I love music. My taste is eclectic.
In fact, I can't think of a type of
    music I don't enjoy.
I even like the driving beat that
    emanates from teenage boom boxes.
Music can drive me or soothe me.

Lord, You are like music in my life.
You are an intense driving force and a
    calming presence.
You are my God during celebration and
    my God during sorrow and grief.
Lord, may all my music be suitable
    praise to You.
May the music I hear fuel me and inspire me
    to a more effective life of service.
Thanks for the gift of joyful music
    and for creating a world
    full of sound. Amen.

# Week 13 Activities

**Themes:** Calm, fear, mentors, music, security, storms

**Old Testament Exploration:** Genesis 32:22–30; Psalm 98

**New Testament Exploration:** Matthew 8:23–27; John 1:35–51

> The knowledge that we are never alone calms the troubled sea of our lives and speaks peace to our souls.
>
> *A. W. Tozer*

> Music is almost all we have of heaven on earth.
>
> *Joseph Addison*

> Do not pray for easy lives,
> Pray to be stronger men.
> Do not pray for tasks equal to your powers,
> Pray for powers equal to your task.
>
> *Phillips Brooks*

## Reflect

Who do you consider your mentor? How do you see God at work in your relationship? List your favorite musical pieces. How do they make you feel? List your favorite hymns. How do they help you express your faith? Pick your favorite hymn and commit it to memory. Teach it to your children and explain its significance.

........................................................

# WEEK 14

*God's riches at Christ's expense.* Take the first letter from each word in that sentence and they spell *grace.* What an amazing God we have. He looked at the sinful worms we are and sent His Son to die on the cross. At Christ's expense, we are saved. We did nothing and can do nothing to merit this gift. Praise God for His wonderful *grace.*

........................................

# Judging Others

*[Jesus said,] "Do not judge, or you too will be judged."*
(*Matthew 7:1*)

It's so easy to judge others.
I do it all the time.
I evaluate people according to my standards.
I wonder why Joe can't be more
    accepting of others, or why Helen can't
    make better use of her time.
There's some pious motives too.
I often ask, "How can *they* call themselves
    Christians and act *that* way?"
In my mind, I've already
    reached a conclusion.

But You want us to turn things
    around.
You want us to look at ourselves and find
    our own faults.
That's where the problem begins, Lord.
One glance in the mirror of Your Law, and I
    turn away. I can't measure up.
What am I to do?
Jesus, Your victory over sin is the
    only solution for me,
    just as it is for others.
Help me as I live under
    Your grace and share Your forgiveness
    with those around me. Amen.

# Grace Applied

*Christ Jesus came into the world to save sinners—of
whom I am the worst. (1 Timothy 1:15)*

Lord I marvel at Paul's honesty—
    especially when he speaks of his past life.
Saul, the persecutor of Christians, became
    Paul, the apostle.
"The grace of our Lord was poured out on me
    abundantly."

I consider my past sins too, Lord,
    and marvel at Your forgiveness.
It's a miracle that You made me part of
    Your family.
"... I was shown mercy so that in me, the
    worst of sinners ..."
I can always depend on Your grace, even
    in this unstable world.

But what is my response to the
    saving faith You've given me?
It can be no less than a full commitment to
    service within Your kingdom.
I should share the message of Your
    grace with others through a
    forgiving lifestyle.
In the midst of my daily routine, help me take
    time to remember whose I am
    and how You made me Your child. Amen.

# Servanthood

Lord, I have an attitude problem.
I feel like I'm being used,
    and I don't like it.
But isn't that the life You've
    called me to live?
How do I function as a servant without
    feeling used?

I don't feel affirmed for the work I do.
Other people seem to get recognition and
    encouragement.
I just feel ignored—unless there's an
    extra task to be done.
And this attitude problem
    snowballs until it affects all
    my relationships, even with those I love.
I don't like what's happening.

Lord, I know You understand.
You came to earth as a servant.
If anyone was taken advantage of, You were.
Even knowing this, I often forget to say thanks.
Instead I take advantage of Your
    benevolent nature.
Remind me that I should imitate You.
And You will supply the strength
    I need to overcome feelings of disapproval.
Help me find satisfaction in You
    and wait for my heavenly reward. Amen.

........................................

# Week 14 Activities

**Themes:** Grace, judgment, reward, servanthood, sin

**Old Testament Exploration:** Isaiah 55:1-7; Micah 4:1-15

**New Testament Exploration:** Matthew 20:25-28; Romans 14:1-23; 1 Timothy 1:12-17

> Do little things as if they were great because of the majesty of the Lord Jesus Christ who dwells in you; and do great things as if they were little and easy because of his omnipotence.
>
> *Blaise Pascal*

> God does not so much need people to do extra-ordinary things as he needs people who do ordinary things extraordinarily well.
>
> *William Barclay*

> The law detects, grace alone conquers sin.
>
> *St. Augustine*

> Forebear to judge, for we are sinners all.
>
> *William Shakespeare*

## Reflect

If God were to measure you by the standards you use to judge others, how would you rank? How, in fact, does God judge you? Thank Him for looking at Jesus' perfect life and His death for you instead of your sin-filled life. How does this free gift of salvation make you feel? What responsibilities does this freedom carry? (See Romans 8:1–17.)

# WEEK 15

Solitude often plays havoc with the human mind. When we're alone, doubt creeps in, and fear drives a wedge between us and God. Jesus relished His time alone because it was then that He talked with His Father. In solitude, God strengthened Him for the road ahead. The next time you're alone, spend time with your heavenly Father. He will remove the wedge of fear and banish any doubts.

.........................................

..........................................

# Saying Good-bye to a Friend

Mark is moving to Indianapolis.
We had a farewell lunch for him today.
We shared some memories, laughed, and
    wished him Godspeed.

Father, I realize all earthly relationships
    are temporary.
Life is a series of transitions,
    hellos and good-byes.
Nothing is permanent, especially friendships.

But Father, I need people.
I need the stability of regular companionship.
I need the security of a support group.
Mark was part of that and he's leaving.
    What if others aren't far behind?

I know You're still in charge, Father.
Friends may move in and out of my life,
    but You are eternal.
Lord, please be a part of my earthly circle
    of friends.
I need You now more than ever. Amen.

......................................

# Doubt

Where did this come from?
I suddenly have doubts about myself.
I'm even questioning Your existence, God.
I can't pinpoint an event that caused this.
    It's just suddenly there.

Lord, I don't like how I'm acting.
    What must it be like for those
    who work and live with me?
I'm not very productive, and
    I can't be much fun to be around.

Straighten me out spiritually, Lord, so
    the pieces of my life fall back
    into place.
Give me trust to let You put me back
    on the right track.
Guide me to passages in Your Word that will
    remind me of Your constant presence and
    desires for my life.

As Your baptized child, daily
    wash away my sin and
    renew a clean spirit within me.
Take away my doubts and restore my faith.
Feed me with Your Word and
    strengthen my relationship with You.
Bring to my heart the joy of Your salvation and
    let it flow through me.
Gather me into Your all-powerful arms. Amen.

# Sleepless Nights

I can't sleep, Lord.
It's 4 A.M., and I've been awake
  for hours.
I'm just sitting here in the family room,
  listening to the quiet.

Something interrupted my sleep,
  but I can't figure out what.
It's not like I can afford to be
  awake in the middle of the night.
My schedule is full, and I need to be
  on my toes at work.
I really need to sleep, but I can't.
So here I sit.

Lord, You're here with me,
  telling me it's time to slow down,
Reminding me it's time we had an
  intimate conversation.
Thanks for reminding me that
  You're here, Father.
Help me place my life in Your hands.
Confident of Your presence, I can rest
  secure—even when I can't sleep. Amen.

............................................

# Week 15 Activities

**Themes:** Comfort, doubt, fear, friendship, sleep, stability, strength

**Old Testament Exploration:** 1 Samuel 20:1–42; Psalm 51

**New Testament Exploration:** Hebrews 11:1–12; James 1:3–12

> A friend will joyfully sing with you when you are on the mountaintop, and silently walk beside you through the valley.
>
> *Anon.*

> Doubt sees the obstacles;
>   faith sees the way.
> Doubt sees the darkest night;
>   faith sees the day.
> Doubt dreads to take a step;
>   faith soars on high;
> Doubt questions, "Who believes?"
>   Faith answers "I."
>
> *Anon.*

> Alone with God! It is there that what is hid with God is made known—God's ideals, God's hopes, God's doings.
>
> *Oswald Chambers*

## Reflect

Who is your best friend? Why? Thank God for this person. How does God work through your best friend, your wife, your family to assuage your doubts and fears? List three things that sometimes keep you up at night. Turn them over to God. He promises never to sleep so that you can.

# WEEK 16

"Yet not as I will, but as You will." What difficult words Jesus spoke in Gethsemane. He knew the betrayal to come. He knew the death to come. But Jesus trusted His Father to strengthen Him for the task. Make this phrase part of your prayer life. God's desires are greater than yours. He will direct you and strengthen you for the path you are to follow.

..........................................

# Gethsemane

*[Jesus said,] "Watch and pray so that you will not fall into temptation." (Matthew 26:41)*

I can learn so many lessons
   from Your prayer in the garden, Jesus.
In Your omniscience, You knew what was ahead.
You went to Gethsemane looking for
   a way out as much as You did
   for strength.
You spent time alone with Your Father.
Even Your best friends fell asleep as the
   hour grew late.

While You struggled with the fate awaiting You,
   the question wasn't what You wanted:
   "Yet not as I will, but as You will."
Jesus, You always prayed like that.
Faced with a difficult task, You sought
   strength and guidance from the
   one source You could depend on—Your
   Father.
Now You could face the betrayal and all
   its implications with
   boldness and confidence.
"Rise, let us go! Here comes My betrayer!"
What a message.
I often come to You, looking for an easy answer,
   an easy out.
Even when the path You have planned is

clear, I try to justify my
    alternative actions.
Jesus, You sought Your Father's will and
    moved forward confidently.
Jesus, give me the faith to
    pray like that. Amen.

# On Trial

*Jesus remained silent.* (*Matthew 26:63*)

Despite the hostile mood, You
    remained in control.
You knew Your fate was sealed before You even
    arrived.
Those present only sought Your extinction.
Yet You didn't strike back.
You spoke only the truth, and even that was
    more than they could handle.

Jesus, I battle my temper constantly.
When I feel threatened, I strike back.
My tongue becomes caustic.
I use any power I have to inflict harm, even
    in hopeless situations.

I react because I lack faith.
I resist any thought that this could be an
    opportunity to practice discipleship.
Surely a loving God wouldn't put me in such a
    situation.
And then, Jesus, there You are,
    in the midst of an angry mob, there because
    You are carrying out Your Father's will.
You challenge me again to consider Your will
    for my life.
As I boldly move forward in my walk of
    discipleship, may I always remember I
    am Your representative to a
    hostile world. Amen.

······································

# Forsaken

*Jesus cried out in a loud voice ... "My God, My God,
why have You forsaken Me?" (Matthew 27:46)*

I want to protect my children from danger.
If they're in trouble, I want to be there,
    to comfort, to help.
That's why these words are so disconcerting.
You were totally alone, Jesus.
Your Father wanted You to die on the cross,
    but then He turned away from You.
The sins You carried, my sins, separated You
    from Your Father.

Throughout Your sacrificial act,
    the weight of all the sins of the
    whole world rested on Your shoulders.
You became an abomination to
    Your dear Father—for me.
I'm overwhelmed.
You experienced hell—separation from God—
    in my place.

Because of what You did, I need never
    face that kind of suffering.
My life is a life of hope and expectation.
Your victory assures my victory.
    I can even face death confidently.
I know You will never forsake me,
    instead You carry me gently in
    Your arms. Amen.

# Week 16 Activities

**Theme:** Jesus

**Old Testament Exploration:** Psalm 22; Isaiah 52:13–53:12

**New Testament Exploration:** Matthew 27:45–56; 1 Peter 2:13–25

> The cross for the first time revealed God in terms of weakness and lowliness and suffering; even, humanly speaking, of absurdity. He was seen thenceforth in the image of the most timid, most gentle, and most vulnerable of all living creatures—a lamb. Agnus Dei!
>
> *Malcolm Muggeridge*

> I remember two things: that I am a great sinner and that Christ is a great Savior.
>
> *John Newton*

> By a Carpenter mankind was made, and only by that Carpenter can mankind be remade.
>
> *Desiderius Erasmus*

## Reflect

Jesus died to take away your sins. What does this mean to you?

# WEEK 17

Jesus lives! The vict'ry's won!
Death no longer can appall me;
Jesus lives! Death's reign is done!
From the grave will Christ recall me.
Brighter scenes will then commence;
This shall be my confidence.

..............................................

# Easter

We've done some dreadful things to
    Your special days, Lord.
Easter could be the prime example.
Instead of Your day of victory, a day
    You want to share with Your people,
    we've turned it into a celebration of
    candy and bunnies.
People dress in their finest clothes,
    to impress others.
We observe the rite of spring, but do we
    celebrate Your defeat of
    sin and the grave?

Unfamiliar faces fill the pews on Easter.
Where are they the rest of the year?
What right do they have to come
    only once a year?
But who am I to complain?
Weren't my sins the reason for the events
    that led to that first Easter?
I should be living a life of celebration
    for the salvation You've given me,
    not just celebrating one day each year.
The thoughts and actions of others shouldn't
    affect me.

Lord, be with me during my Easter celebration.
May the joy of Your Easter victory show
    in all that I say and do.
Use me, Lord, to bring others to the
    celebration of Your Easter triumph. Amen.

........................................

# Morning

I love mornings. I especially love
    spring mornings.
The fresh air gives me a natural high.
Just getting the newspaper
    rejuvenates me.

I hear some people say
    they hate mornings.
That must make their days difficult.
It must make facing each day
    a chore,
    like there's nothing to live for.

There have been times when I
    hated mornings.
I was in a rut. I felt sorry for myself.
Mornings became difficult for me too.

That's why I appreciate Your love so much,
    Lord.
Through the gift of Your Son, each
    morning is a new day.
I'm a baptized child of God. My
    sins are forgiven, and I
    begin each day anew.

Thanks for mornings. Thanks, too, for my
    change in attitude.
Thanks especially for the gift of Jesus.
    He makes each morning, each day, special.
Help me live today showing that
    I believe. Amen.

························

# Victory

*The angel said to the women, "... He is not here; He has risen, just as He said." (Matthew 28:5–6)*

Victory!
You had accomplished what You set out to do,
    Jesus.
You defeated sin and death.
The tomb was empty.

Why do people need to explain
    Your resurrection, Lord?
Why do we struggle to understand what we
    should accept on faith?
We develop theories about the earthquake.
We debate the location of the tomb and the
    authenticity of a burial shroud.
Why do we need to understand?
It should be enough to know
    You are alive and
    Your victory is ours.

"Greetings," You said to the women.
And You come to me with the
    same words each day.
Jesus, assure me of Your presence.
Comfort me with Your gentle command,
    "Don't be afraid."
Challenge me with Your commission,
    "Go and tell!"

Lord, help me react in faith to
    the news of Your resurrection and

avoid the need to "prove" it.
Accept my thanks and praise as I
    daily celebrate Your presence in my life.
Let my faith be a light on the hill for
    those I come in contact with. Amen.

..........................................

# Week 17 Activities

**Themes:** Easter, hope, joy, life, love, resurrection

**Old Testament Exploration:** Psalm 91; Isaiah 60:1–7

**New Testament Exploration:** John 20:1–18; 1 Peter 1:3–12

> Our Lord has written the promise of the resurrection not in books alone, but in every leaf in springtime.
>
> *Martin Luther*

> The day of resurrection!
> Earth, tell it out abroad,
> The passover of gladness,
> The passover of God.
> From death to life eternal,
> From sin's dominion free,
> Our Christ has brought us over
> With hymns of victory.
>
> *St. John of Damascus*

## Reflect

Read 1 Corinthians 15:13–20, 42–44, 54–57. Thank God that your faith is not in vain. The victory is yours through Christ.

# WEEK 18

A busy hum fills most workplaces. In fact, if it's too quiet, we question whether anyone's working. But God works quietly. A seed is planted. It's watered by His Word. It's nurtured by His Supper. It ripens and bears fruit. It spreads to fertile ground around it. God uses simple, ordinary actions and things to accomplish His purposes. Praise Him for His work in your life.

........................................

# My Baptism Day

Father, I'm really embarrassed.
We were talking in Bible class today about
    Baptism.
Someone asked me when my
    Baptism birthday was,
    and I didn't know.
I know I'm Your child, but I don't remember
    the day that it happened.

Perhaps my experience is symptomatic.
We take our citizenship in Your kingdom
    for granted.
I know I was baptized, but it's not something
    I celebrate each year,
    much less daily.
Yet the benefits of Baptism are there for me
    every day, whether I acknowledge them
    or not.
I live under the abiding presence of Your
    grace and mercy.
I ask for forgiveness, sometimes casually,
    and it's always granted.

Lord, may this new awareness create a
    change in my heart.
Your baptismal covenant with me is the most
    important thing in my life.
My future is guaranteed.
I am Your child today and always. Amen.

# Spring

I mowed the lawn for the first time
    this spring.
Come June and July, yard work will be
    a chore, but today it was
    great to be outside.
Thanks for the smell of fresh-cut grass, Lord.

The warm breezes of spring, after the
    cold winds of winter, are like a
    smooth cup of coffee—a warmth that
    spreads through my whole body.
Buds form on flowers and trees.
Soon the whole countryside will be decked
    in green.
Longer days mean more time outside,
    more time for family.
Lord, make this a great spring and summer.

Spring brings a new spirit and
    joy to my winter-dulled life.
Lord, help me realize that the spirit of spring
    isn't limited to one season.
The gift of Your Son means new
    life every day.
His resurrection one spring morning
    changed the course of history.
    And it changed my life.
Every day becomes a celebration of
    our victory through Jesus.

Father, thanks for spring and the
    reminder of Your most important gift. Amen.

# A Walk in the Park

I enjoy walking.
   It's probably the best exercise for me.
And there's a walking path so close to
   our home.
Great exercise that's convenient—
   you can't beat that.

Some people walk with
   headphones on, listening to music,
   catching up on the news.
I enjoy listening to the
   sounds of Your world, Father.
The wind through the trees and the sweet
   serenade of the birds,
They remind me of Your presence.

But it's the conversations that
   I have with You that I enjoy the most.
You walk along with me, Father,
   and we talk about my life.
It encourages me to know You always listen.
The responses I see in my life
   motivate me to keep talking.
Walking refreshes me.
But is it the physical
   or the spiritual exercise
   that does me more good, Father?

Lord, continue to walk with me as I
   exercise body and soul. Amen.

# Week 18 Activities

**Themes:** Baptism, nature, new life, prayer, spring

**Old Testament Exploration:** Exodus 15:1–21; Psalm 33

**New Testament Exploration:** Galatians 3:26–4:7;
1 John 2:7–14

> Every April God rewrites the book of Genesis.
>
> *Anon.*

> But I would want—and this is my daily prayer—
> that I might duly honor and truly esteem the gift
> of my Baptism and thank God for it.
>
> *Martin Luther*

> Nature is the art of God Eternal.
>
> *Dante Alighieri*

## Reflect

When were you baptized? Do you celebrate this "birthday"? Mark your entire family's Baptism days on a calendar. Celebrate the day with a cake, a present, and a prayer of thanks to God for His gift of faith.

# W E E K  1 9

How often do you come home from work and tell your kids you'll do something with them later? Do you follow through? Make time now for your children. Play with them. Help them with schoolwork. Have a daily devotion with them. Sit with your kids in church and help them participate. Pray for them. Train them in God's ways. Ask God to help you be a Christian father.

..........................................

# A Sleeping Child

Father, tonight I stood and watched
   as she slept.
I'm still in awe of Your creation,
   that You have
   entrusted her to our care.

As she lay there tonight,
   she changed before my eyes.
No longer a little girl,
   with every stretch and subtle move,
   she seemed to grow.

I believe her stretches
   indicate the struggles within.
The transition from childhood to adulthood
   is traumatic.
I don't need to be reminded.
I see it daily as I watch her grapple
   with decisions and changing relationships.

The tension exists in our relationship.
   It changes constantly.
At times, she pushes my patience
   to the limit.
Through it all, however, she remains
   my daughter.

Father, give me wisdom and patience
   to meet her needs.
Make me a courageous father who lovingly
   takes a stand on the issues but

continues to encourage and support exploration and growth.

I know she needs me now more than ever. Enable me to be there for her, just as You are always there for me. Amen.

# The School Musical

Lord, it's spring musical time again.
That means enduring the fray as
    parents scramble for the best seats.
That means straining to catch a glimpse of
    my kids amidst all the video cameras.

This night is important to the kids.
They've worked hard, and Katie makes
    a cute cowgirl.
And Mark has the opportunity to
    sing—and singing in front of people
    improves his self-confidence.

Father, You give us all kinds of talents and
    the opportunities to use them.
Help me view school musicals as one such
    opportunity.
Maybe I'd rather see Mark hit a
    winning home run, but developing
    his musical talent is important too.

Lord, as I look at our children, I see lots of
    talent and lots of promise.
Make them good managers of all that
    You have given them.
Through Your Spirit, enable me to model
    the proper use of Your gifts.
Help me as a parent to be an encourager,
    not a meddler.

My kids' achievements are gifts from You.
    May You be praised. Amen.

..........................................

# My Daughter's Birthday

Today is Katie's birthday.
She's looked forward to this day
    for a long time.
There will be gifts, of course, and
    her favorite meal, and a party with
    her friends.
What simple things satisfy a child.

For children, birthdays are a big deal.
They find such joy in living.
Turning older means growing up …
    moving closer to realizing special dreams.
Maybe that's why some adults struggle with
    birthdays—living has become a drudgery and
    we seem to keep moving farther from
    our childhood dreams.

Father, help me rejoice in Katie's dreams
    and help her make them a reality.
Remind me that I need to
    look to You for guidance in my own life.
I need to set goals that agree with
    Your plan for me.
It is Your gifts that make those
    dreams possible.
Make me thankful for dreams, both
    those I've attained and those I'm
    still moving toward.

Thank You for the gift of
    childish excitement and anticipation. Amen.

# Week 19 Activities

**Themes:** Birthdays, children, decisions, fatherhood, growing up, performing, talents

**Old Testament Exploration:** Genesis 17:15–22; Deuteronomy 6:1–9

**New Testament Exploration:** Mark 5:21–43; Titus 2:1–15

> The best way for a child to learn to fear God is to know a real Christian. The best way for a child to learn to pray is to live with a father and mother who know a life of friendship with God and who truly pray.
>
> *Johann H. Pestalozzi*

> The Lord made Adam from the dust of the earth, but when the first toddler came along, he added electricity!
>
> *Anon.*

## Reflect

Go into your children's rooms tonight and watch them sleep. Ask God to watch and care for them. What talents has God given to your children? How do you help them make the most of these talents? Make your child's next birthday special by giving him or her a card with a note that you say a prayer for them every day. Make sure this is a truthful statement!

........................................................

# W E E K   2 0

Our society caters to the impatient. There's fast-food, drive-up pharmacies, one-hour photo shops, express lanes, microwaves—an endless list. God's idea of "speedy" is thousands of years spent waiting for the Savior. When we ask God for something, we want an immediate answer. But God provides His perfect answer at the best time—whether that's right away or 40 years from now.

..............................................

..............................................

# Waiting

Airport lounges, dentist offices,
    supermarket checkout lines—
    I spend a lot of my time
    waiting.
And waiting seems like a waste of time.
I think of the things I could be
    doing if I wasn't waiting.
And I get frustrated.

Scripture reminds me that
    waiting is a part of Your plan, Father.
I complain about a 30-minute wait because
    my flight is delayed;
I can't imagine waiting 40 years to
    reach the Promised Land or
    2,000 years for my Savior.

You have Your reasons for making waiting
    a part of my life.
I should accept it and
    find ways to make it productive.

Lord, help me constructively use my
    time spent waiting.
Clear my mind and focus my thoughts on You.
Remind me that the longest
    wait is already over.
    I know I have a Savior.
Encourage me to spread the Good News as
    I wait. Amen.

............................................

# Patience

I've always placed patience at the top of
my prayer list.
But lately, Lord, I've wondered if I'm
praying for the right thing.
I might be more patient, but am I
using "patience" to avoid facing
difficult tasks?

Patience is a spiritual gift—a
desired trait—especially when it comes to
waiting for You to act.
But is patience always the
right response in earthly relationships?
Doesn't my patience sometimes indicate an
unwillingness to change a bad situation?
Can't it become a crutch, a means of
holding me back from doing what I know
is right?

I still need to work on patience in
some areas of my life.
But when it comes to defending You,
protecting my family,
keeping myself out of sin's way,
I need to be a man of action.

Lord, grant me the wisdom to know where
action or patience should be practiced.
Give me the courage and strength to
act swiftly when necessary.
Make me a daring disciple in all situations,
willing to exhibit the faith
You have given me. Amen.

# The Report

It started as a simple report, but
   it has upended our house for days.
It was supposed to involve some research
   and then some typing.
It sounded simple, but then other kids' parents
   started adding to it.
What began as extra credit became a
   requirement.
Now our dining-room table looks like a
   physics lab.

Lord, I know the high value of education, but
   I really think we'd be better off
   letting our children work on their own.
Now our house is in an uproar because
   other parents weren't willing to
   stay out of their kids' schoolwork.
And we followed along and allowed
   the assignment to consume our lives too.

Father, I want our children to be successful.
   Their education is a top priority.
But I need help keeping it in perspective.
It is, after all, supposed to be
   their experience, not mine.
And I never want them to think my happiness
   is based on their success.
Father, remind me to keep Your
   message of love and salvation, and Your
   desires for us, ever before my children.
That needs to be part of their learning
   experience too. Amen.

........................................

# Week 20 Activities

**Themes:** Education, patience, waiting

**Old Testament Exploration:** Exodus 34:1-9; Job 1:6-22

**New Testament Exploration:** Romans 15:1-13; James 5:7-12

> Teach us, O Lord, the disciplines of patience, for to wait is often harder than to work.
>
> *Peter Marshall*

> No one will ever know the full depth of his capacity for patience and humility as long as nothing bothers him. It is only when times are troubled and difficult that he can see how much of either is in him.
>
> *St. Francis of Assisi*

> Integrity without knowledge is weak and useless, and knowledge without integrity is dangerous and dreadful.
>
> *Samuel Johnson*

## Reflect

Think about the times you've needed patience. Has your ability to wait improved or gotten worse over the years? Ask God to guide your actions and improve your patience. What importance do you place on education? Thank God for the talents He has given you in the arena of academics.

......................................................

# WEEK 21

On the seventh day, God rested. When do you rest? Some men think they're stronger than God. They work 60-hour weeks and play hard on the weekends. Rare vacations become marathon trips to dozens of sites. God rested, why can't you? Go camping. Take your wife on a picnic. Take your kids to the zoo. Take a daily walk and talk with God. Ask Him to bless your leisure time.

......................................................

........................................

# Fair Day

Father, today is one of my favorite
    days of the whole year.
It's fair day, and I get to spend it with
    my favorite people—my kids.
I love the sights, the sounds, the smells
    of the fair.
I especially love the tastes—
    funnel cakes, corn dogs, and
    barbecued turkey legs.

The fair takes me back to my childhood—and
    fair days spent with my parents.
We get to see a cross-sectional view of life.
The farmer, the merchant, and the manufacturer
    join together to display their wares.
People of all races, colors, and economic
    strata come to have fun.

Lord, make this a great day.
Keep us safe. Help us learn.
    Let us have fun together.
    Bless our family time.
And Lord, thanks for going with us to
    the fair. Amen.

# Memorial Day

Many folks look forward to this day
  all winter.
It marks the beginning of summer.
But wouldn't it be more appropriate to
  move Memorial Day to another time,
  perhaps when the weather was
  cold and damp?
What's supposed to be a day of
  solemn remembrance is celebrated with
  picnics and swimming parties.

I recall a trip to Arlington National
  Cemetery, seeing row after row of white
  crosses, and realizing the great price paid to
  ensure our freedom.
Are today's partyers aware of our
  history? Do they even know what
  they're observing?

But what about me?
Your Son paid a great price to win
  my freedom from sin, and
  I daily abuse this freedom.
Yet You forgive me over and over again.
I live not only as a citizen of this country
  but as part of Your kingdom.
I'm doubly blessed.

Make me a responsible citizen of
  both kingdoms—one who truly
  appreciates and remembers the
  freedom fighters. Amen.

........................................

# Friends

I had breakfast with my friends
    this morning.
It was just the usual sharing, Bible study,
    and prayer time.
But I left without thanking them for their
    friendship.

Lord, I couldn't make it without my friends.
    They support, encourage, and pray for me.
They are Your representatives in my life.
There are times I share things with them that
    no one else knows.

When we're together as friends,
    I feel Your presence.
You're right there in the middle of our group.
You are the Friend who binds us together,
    friends on earth but brothers in Christ.

Loving Father, thanks for the gift of
    friendship.
More important, thanks for the gift
    of Your Son, the greatest Friend of all. Amen.

# Week 21 Activities

**Themes:** Childhood, freedom, friendship, fun, Memorial Day

**Old Testament Exploration:** Proverbs 17:17; Ecclesiastes 4:1–12

**New Testament Exploration:** Romans 8:12–17

> Words cannot express the joy which a friend imparts; they only can know who have experienced that joy. A friend is dearer than the light of heaven, for it would be better for us that the sun were extinguished than that we should be without friends.
>
> *John Chrysostom*

> Memory tempers prosperity, mitigates adversity, controls youth, and delights old age.
>
> *Anon.*

> Acquire enthusiasm; you can't be enthusiastic and unhappy at the same time.
>
> *Anon.*

## Reflect

List five things you value about your friendships. How does God strengthen you through your friends? What things do you enjoy doing? Why? Make plans to do something special with your wife that you both enjoy. Thank God for the time to enjoy life.

# W E E K   2 2

A workshop leader suggested that once a year our confession of faith should include statements of belief in Jesus' miracles. He said it seems easier to confess belief in Jesus' resurrection than in His power to make five loaves and two fish feed more than 5,000 people. Ask God to strengthen your faith in His miraculous power. List the miracles God has worked in your life.

...........................................

# Building a Foundation

*"Yet [the house] did not fall, because it had its foundation on the rock." (Matthew 7:25)*

I'm just back from a servant event.
We built a house.
When we arrived, there was only a
    foundation.
It looked plain and simple, but as I
    reflect, I appreciate its importance.
Without that foundation, the walls we built
    would collapse.
The entire structure rests on the foundation.

Jesus, Your parable provides an example of the
    results of a poor foundation, but I wish
    You'd taken it a step further.
The foundation needs a little maintenance.

You are my faith's foundation,
    but the relationship needs constant upkeep.
You must strengthen that relationship every day.
Study of Your Word,
    participation in Your Supper,
    fellowship with Christian friends,
    and prayer—through these activities,
    You maintain the foundation of my faith.
Jesus, I want to stand firm when
    the storms of life come.
Through the power of Your Spirit, help me
    grow in my relationship with You. Amen.

# Ascension

Today, we celebrate Jesus' ascension.
I wasn't aware of it when I woke up
    this morning,
A colleague reminded me as we
    finished staff devotions.

Jesus, today is the celebration of Your
    return to Your Father in heaven.
You had completed Your earthly task.
The victory was Yours.
But now, almost 2,000 years later, we often
    forget to celebrate Your ascension.

Ascension Day, like All Saints' Day and other
    festivals, used to be special celebrations.
Christians stopped their normal activity to
    worship, remember, and reflect.

No one wished me a "Happy Ascension Day"
    today.
I didn't receive any Ascension Day cards.
I acknowledged this day, not with worship
    and celebration, but with a brief prayer.

Jesus, more than anyone, You know
    the sweat, tears, and pain that
    preceded Ascension Day.
Always keep before me the glory of this day.
Your job was done.
My salvation was won.
Thank You. Amen.

........................................

# Pentecost

What a tremendous worship
   service we had today in
   Your house—incredible music and a
   personally inspiring message.
I really appreciated hearing the
   Pentecost story again.

Lord, through the power of Your Spirit,
   You work powerful things
   in and through people.
I marvel at the changes in Peter and the
   other disciples.
From cowering in darkened rooms to
   preaching boldly throughout the city,
   You transformed the lives of
   Your followers.
To think that You brought
   thousands into Your family through
   Baptism in one day
   astounds me.

The world still thirsts for Your message.
Instead of a church boldly
   proclaiming Your saving power, it seems
   too wrapped up in political issues to
   fulfill Your commission.
Lord, forgive us.

Pour Your Spirit on us again.
Awaken in us an overwhelming zeal to
   spread Your Word to the nations.

Renew us and bless our efforts to
 serve You.

Make us powerful witnesses to Your name.
 Amen.

......................................

# Week 22 Activities

**Themes:** Ascension, change, foundation, Pentecost, praise, worship

**Old Testament Exploration:** Psalm 24:7–10; Ezekiel 37:1–14; Joel 2:28–32

**New Testament Exploration:** Acts 1:1–11; Ephesians 1:1–23

> Jesus departed from our sight that he might return to our heart. He departed, and behold, he is here.
>
> *St. Augustine*

> Wherever the Son of God goes, the winds of God are blowing, the streams of living water are flowing, and the sun of God is smiling.
>
> *Helmut Thielicke*

## Reflect

Write down what you believe about Jesus Christ. How do the events of Ascension and Pentecost support and strengthen this statement? How has the Holy Spirit worked in your life to make it possible for you to write this statement? Take time on both Ascension and Pentecost to praise God for His plan of salvation and for the faith He has given to you.

# WEEK 23

The simplest things often have great significance. Consider the importance of wood, water, and flour. On the wooden cross, Christ died to save you. In Baptism, God used simple water combined with His Word to make you His child. In the Lord's Supper, through the wine, bread, and His Word, God gives you forgiveness and strength. Thank Him for His simple gifts.

............................................................

# Coffee

Someone forgot to make the coffee.
I arrived to find people waiting by the
    coffee pot.
They were waiting for the signal that
    the coffee is brewed and work can begin.

Lord, I'll admit that I'm among the worst
    offenders when it comes to coffee.
But it provides a pick-me-up.
My mind seems sharper, and I'm more on
    top of things.

But Lord, as I think about it, why do I need
    to drink something to feel that way?
Why does too much coffee make me feel
    uptight?
All that coffee can't be good for me.

Lord, help me drink coffee responsibly,
    like I do other beverages.
Help me avoid using it as a stimulant
    and crutch.
Remind me that real rejuvenation is
    only found in You. Amen.

........................................

# Violence

It seemed so distant.
My experiences with violence came
    via television or newspaper reports.
Then it hit close to home.
A friend was beaten and robbed in a
    parking lot.
He's recovering physically,
    but I'm not sure he or anyone
    close to him will be the same
    emotionally.

It's hard to understand the
    motivation for violence.
But it's always been around—from
    Cain and Abel through Jeremiah, and
    it even touched You, Lord.
One of Your parables even addressed it, the one
    about the man on the trip to Jericho.

The reality of violence doesn't make it
    easier to accept—or change.
Robbery and murder aren't in Your plan for us.
They're part of a sinful world.
And sin seems to breed sin.
    Violence holds people hostage,
    afraid to speak out or get
    involved in prevention.
We keep our heads down and
    our ears closed to cries for help.

Despite what's happening around us,
    help me provide a secure

haven for my family.
From this safe harbor,
    guide us, Lord, as we work to
    spread the message of peace
    through Your Son. Amen.

............................................

# Meetings

Lord, here I sit.
To be honest, I've been sitting in this
    same place for more than two hours.
I've consumed too much coffee, and my
    backside is sore.
I hope others don't see me squirming as I try
    to stay awake.
It seems I spend too much of my time
    in meetings.
Planning and decision-making are part of the
    process,
But is this particular meeting
    the best use of my time?

Lord, when You call a meeting, it tends to be
    a "one on one" encounter, like
    with Moses on Mount Sinai.
You are a God of action.
    You speak, and things happen.

Perhaps if our leaders sought
    to do Your will, we would
    have fewer meetings.
Until then I'll have to endure them.
Lord, enable me to be Your voice in
    this meeting.
Empower me to use my "meeting" time to
    benefit Your kingdom. Amen.

..........................................

# Week 23 Activities

**Themes:** Character, conscience, difficulties, discipline, violence

**Old Testament Exploration:** Genesis 18:1–10

**New Testament Exploration:** Luke 10:30–37;
2 Corinthians 6:1–10

> God brings problems and struggles into our lives so that we will not stray from the main road. He is not angry with us but disciplines us so that we can mature spiritually.
>
> *Erwin W. Lutzer*

> Returning violence for violence multiplies violence, adding deeper darkness to a night already devoid of stars.
>
> *Martin Luther King Jr.*

## Reflect

What artificial "crutches" do you depend on in your life? How can God help you place your trust firmly in Him? How does your faith provide security in these violent times?

# WEEK 24

Consider the importance of your family. How does God work through these people to strengthen you? Write a note to the family member who is your spiritual mentor. Thank that person for making or keeping God the focus of your life. Write a note to wife. List the reasons she's a gift from God. Write notes to your children. Make sure they know you pray for them.

.............................................

# Fathering

Lord, one word overwhelms me
    personally.
It's *father*.
I guess it overwhelms me
    because in Your prayer, You
    give us permission to call
    You *Father*.

When I think of the perfect Father that You are,
    I know I can never measure up.
You are unfailingly loving and compassionate.
You continually provide us with all we need,
    even though we don't deserve it.
I can never be as patient as You.

But You have called me to be a father.
Your domain is great, mine is rather
    small.
Yet to some people, I'm very important.
I'm their *father*.

Give me the wisdom, strength, and insight
    I need to be a good father.
Through the gift of Your Spirit, help me
    model You in all things.
And be patient with me when I come up short.

Lord, especially help me to be
    forgiving toward my family.
May my forgiveness know no bounds, just as
    Your forgiveness washes
    away all my sins. Amen.

# Family First

*A deacon must be the husband of but one wife and must manage his children and his household well. (1 Timothy 3:12)*

These words invoke such
    guilt within me.
I've fallen short of Your expectations,
    Father.
I've neglected my duty.
At times my job has come before
    my own household.

It can't continue this way.
I need You in our home, just as
    You touch other aspects of my life.
You are the true head of our family.
As Lord of my life, guide me as
    I lead my family in dedicated
    service to You.

Father, forgive me for the
    times I fail to follow Your path.
Give my entire family a
    forgiving spirit toward one another.
Help us each to live our lives as
    servants.

Lord, come and be a part of our home.
May our meal time and play time
    and all time be a
    celebration of Your existence. Amen.

# Baseball

Father, thanks for baseball.
I love the game for its simplicity.
The green grass, the bright sunshine, the
    roar of the crowd—it exhilarates me.
I enjoy watching baseball on TV after a
    long day. It's great relaxation.
But I'm strictly a spectator.
Getting up from my chair takes effort.
I like observing from the dugout.
    Let me strategize and second-guess
    the manager.

You created all things, so
    baseball must be part of Your plan.
Some players even share Your message.
While some people are taken aback
    at that, I appreciate it.
    We need all the positive role models
    we can get.
Baseball is definitely our family game.
    I love sharing it with my children.

Lord, thanks again for baseball.
Thanks for a means to enjoy life and
    spend quality time with my family. Amen.

# Week 24 Activities

**Themes:** Family, fatherhood, quality time, rest, sports

**Old Testament Exploration:** Exodus 20:12; Psalm 68:1–6

**New Testament Exploration:** Ephesians 6:4; Colossians 3:21

> A happy family is but an earlier heaven.
>
> *Sir John Bowring*

> Every word and deed of a parent is a fibre woven into the character of a child that ultimately determines how that child fits into the fabric of society.
>
> *David Wilkerson*

> Let everyone know, therefore, that it is his duty, on peril of losing the divine favor, to bring up his children above all things in the fear and knowledge of God and, if they are talented, to let them learn and study so that they may be of service wherever they are needed.
>
> *Martin Luther*

## Reflect

What importance do you place on your family, especially your children? Do you take seriously God's commands about bringing up children? Do you turn to God regularly for help? List three things you need to work on as a father and/or husband. Ask God to help you in these areas.

# WEEK 25

Human relationships require time and shared experiences to solidify the bond of love and respect. The same goes for your relationship with God. Do you spend time studying His Word? Do you talk with Him daily? Do you give Him the opportunity to strengthen the bond of faith through participation in worship and the Lord's Supper? Ask God to help you treasure your relationship with Him

# Our Silver Anniversary

It doesn't seem possible that we've
   been married for 25 years.
I still remember our wedding day.
   It rained.
The only bright spot was
   seeing my bride walk down the aisle.

The years have not always been easy.
We've laughed together
   and cried together.
We've shared in the financial and
   personal struggles.
Sometimes there's been
   more sickness than health.

We talked about a trip or perhaps a
   party for our friends on our 25th.
Instead, it's a day like any other.
Even a dinner alone will come when
   it's convenient.

Lord, we don't need all the other things.
We have each other
   and our family,
   and You in the middle of it all.
You have blessed us immeasurably by
   giving us each other.
You make our relationship work.

Father, Your love dwells here.

Your grace is part of our lives.
Your forgiving hand touches us daily—
  Hurts are forgiven,
  shortcomings overlooked,
  feelings respected.
Thanks for 25 years of a great marriage! Amen.

# Rain

The sound came in the night,
   not accompanied by the expected
   crash of thunder but as a
   gentle tapping on the roof.
After weeks of drought, it was raining.

Now the moisture falls in a
   gentle drizzle, a wet caress on my face
   as I venture out to get the morning paper.
I think I hear the plants
   shouting for joy.

Lord, thanks for the rain, but why did it
   take so long?
Everything was suffering—the plants and
   animals and even normally patient
   people had become crabby and worn out.
The heat and dryness took its toll.
But again You responded in Your time,
   in a calm, gentle way.

That's the way You are—responsive to needs
   but when Your time is right.
This rain reinforces that lesson.
Remind me again to wait on You, with
   confidence.
You will respond and Your response brings
   newness of life and hope for the future.

Lord, let Your blessings rain upon me. Amen.

# Relationships

*[Jesus said,] "Whoever does the will of My Father in heaven is My brother and sister and mother."*
(*Matthew 12:50*)

There was a time when I read Your words
    and got upset with You.
At first reading, You seem to be telling me
    to reject my family.
But they are my flesh and blood.
    How can I do that?

As I consider it now, I see You were
    making a point about earthly
    relationships.
They aren't as important
    as our relationship with You.
Your compassion extended beyond Your family
    to Your friends and even to strangers.
You came to save all people.

And the message of salvation through You
    needs to be told.
You have given me the commission to
    tell it to others.
Jesus, help me prioritize my life and
    maintain a healthy relationship
    with You.
Through Your Holy Spirit,
    call me into Your family and
    strengthen me for the jobs You give me.
    Amen.

......................................

# Week 25 Activities

**Themes:** Blessings, faith, family, gifts, love, marriage, promises, support

**Old Testament Exploration:** Genesis 2:18–24; 8:20–22

**New Testament Exploration:** John 2:1–11; Ephesians 5:21–33

> He who does not honor his wife dishonors himself.
>
> *Spanish proverb*

> Successful marriage is always a triangle: a man, a woman, and God.
>
> *Cecil Myers*

> Reflect upon your present blessings of which every man has many; not on your past misfortunes of which all men have some.
>
> *Charles Dickens*

## Reflect

What does your wife mean to you? (If you aren't married, what does your closest friend, girlfriend, or favorite family member mean to you?) What steps have you taken in your marriage to "make things work"? How is God the third side of your marriage triangle? How does your marriage relationship witness your faith to others?

# WEEK 26

"Follow me!" Countless generals have yelled those words. And their armies obeyed. Sometimes the result was victory, sometimes death. Jesus, our spiritual General, calls us to follow Him. But He's already won the battle. Through faith, we are participants in His death and resurrection—His victory over sin, death, and Satan. Thank God that He has made you a follower of Christ.

...........................................

# Spiritual Fitness

It's so easy to go astray.
Other voices call to me—
    myths, old wives' tales, science.
They subvert me into disregard for
    Your Word.
Listening to them takes me
    away from You, Lord.

Paul tells Timothy that
    training for godliness is better than
    mere physical training.
Lord, this training is more than
    Bible study, isn't it?
It includes living a disciplined lifestyle.
It means depending on the
    Holy Spirit's guidance and
    placing myself in His hands to
    nurture and mold me as a
    follower of Christ.

O Holy Spirit, enter my life and
    renew me.
Through Your power, enable me to
    discover all my talents and abilities
    and use them for the good of the kingdom.
With God's Word as my secure footing,
    help me rise above the teachings and
    myths of this world.
Focus me on the true Word—Jesus.
    Challenge me to share the
    message of salvation. Amen.

# Independence Day

It's a national holiday, the day
  we celebrate our freedom.
Today, I also reflect on the freedom
  I have under the Gospel.
What a gift to experience both
  political and spiritual freedom!

Lord, guide my celebration so I am aware of
  the link between these two freedoms.
Our forefathers sought to
  guarantee religious freedom—one of the
  reasons many had come to America.
Now we take it for granted.
Many "Christians" neglect their
  right to worship.
And many "practicing" Christians never
  exercise the freedom to share their faith.

Lord, thank You for the privilege of
  living in a free country.
Help me use my freedoms responsibly.
My gratitude is inexpressible for the
  freedom from sin's bondage Your Son
  won for me.
Keep the joy that Good News brings
  alive in my heart.
Send Your Holy Spirit to guide me as
  You present opportunities to
  share the message of freedom in Jesus.
I want to daily celebrate the
  dual citizenship You have given me. Amen.

# The Call

*"Follow Me," [Jesus] told him. (Matthew 9:9)*

Jesus, You set an example when You
    called Matthew.
Prominent members of the community took
    exception.
    They knew his former occupation.
But You saw Matthew,
    a person in need of forgiveness.
    A person with a job to do in Your kingdom.

You have called me.
There are those who find that
    hard to comprehend.
They see my faults and shortcomings and
    wonder
    how You could use me.
But You see someone in need of love
    and forgiveness.
Someone with a job to do for You.

You came to Matthew personally.
You spoke with him, called him, and ate dinner
    with him and his friends.
You come to me personally.
You join me in quiet times, in the car, at work,
    and even at my meals.
You are a part of my entire life.

You made Matthew the tax collector and sinner
    a disciple.
You made me the sinner a disciple too.

May that discipleship fill every
    aspect of my life as teacher,
    administrator, writer, husband,
    and father.
Help me seek ways to share Your love. Amen.

# Week 26 Activities

**Themes:** Discipleship, faith, freedom, witness

**Old Testament Exploration:** 2 Chronicles 7:11–22;
Psalm 119:33–48

**New Testament Exploration:** Galatians 5:1–15;
Hebrews 11:11–19

> The rule that governs my life is this: Anything that
> dims my vision of Christ, or takes away my taste
> for Bible study, or cramps my prayer life, or
> makes Christian work difficult, is wrong for me,
> and I must, as a Christian, turn away from it.
>
> *J. Wilbur Chapman*

> The God who gave us life, gave us liberty at the
> same time.
>
> *Thomas Jefferson*

## Reflect

Consider for a moment life in a country without
freedom of religion. Would you still worship God?
Would you put your life on the line? Ask the Holy Spirit to strengthen your faith and prepare you daily to witness to what you believe. During this week include a
special prayer of thanks for a country founded on freedom. Ask God to be with our political leaders.

# WEEK 27

Jesus was never too busy to minister to the
crowds that followed Him. He fed them. He
healed them. He talked with them, and He taught
them. How do you spend your time? Do you
ignore opportunities to help others? Do you
avoid worship to play golf or sleep in? Do you
make time for family devotions and recreation?
Ask God to guide you as you plan your schedule.

..........................................

..............................................

# Schedule

I can't handle all the demands being
    put on me.
My daily agenda has become so full that
    things are out of control.
But I don't know how to
    cut back on my obligations.

Unfortunately, my family ends up
    losing.
As much as I try to make time for them,
    something always gets in the way.
It shows. I feel like a stranger
    in my own home.

My job is important.
    I need it to support us.
I'm also proud of what I do.
My success builds up my self-esteem.
But there has to be a balance.

My involvement at church is important.
    The board counts on me for leadership.
I enjoy coaching Little League,
    and our quiet nights out.
But does all this mean I'm overcommitted?

Lord, help me get things under control.
Give me the wisdom to know when to say no
    and the patience to live with
    my many responsibilities. Amen.

# Aging

Eternal Father, I'm getting old.
My body ages, and I find new aches
    every day.
Walking has replaced basketball as exercise.
Aging might be part of Your plan, Lord,
    but it's hard to accept that I can't
    do things that I used to.
Coaching Little League now means
    teaching from the sidelines
    rather than pitching.
Even picking up a golf ball requires
    extra effort.
I remind myself that aging is an
    indication of my sinful nature,
    but that doesn't make it easier.
I still have to accept that I'm
    past my prime.

You've placed a new purpose in my life, Lord.
My daughter's hugs and my sons' smiles
    infuse me with their youthfulness.
My children constantly remind me that
    I'm important to them.
Maybe that's the up side of aging—a
    new appreciation for relationships.
I treasure the time I spend with
    people—especially my family.

Lord, grant me maturity as I age.
Help me age gracefully so that
    youthful joy shines through older eyes. Amen.

# Compassion

*When He saw the crowds, He had compassion on them. (Matthew 9:36)*

Is it just me or are there more
  people on the streets begging?
It seems they stand at every intersection
  with their Will Work for Food signs.
It bothers me most when it's
  mothers with young children.
It's tough to drive by.
    I want to help,
    but I can't help everyone.
I want to meet their needs
    but not encourage their
    lifestyle.

I balance these feelings until I read
  Your Gospel.
Jesus, You had compassion on all humanity,
  not just a select few.
You saw a need and reacted immediately.

Jesus, Your acts of compassion
  express Your infinite love,
  an infinite love You also have
  shown to me.
Because You live in my heart,
  I have an all-powerful love
  to share with others.

Lead me to respond in love to those around me.
Remind me I always have something to

give even when my wallet is empty—
the precious Gospel message.
Send Your Spirit to work through
my smile and words of comfort.
May those in need see
You in me and through me feel
Your love for them. Amen.

# Week 27 Activities

**Themes:** Aging, compassion, maturity, priorities, time

**Old Testament Exploration:** Nehemiah 9:16–21; Ecclesiastes 3:1–8

**New Testament Exploration:** Matthew 9:35–38; Philippians 3:10–16

> Time is a precious gift of God; so precious that he only gives it to us moment by moment.
>
> *Amelia Edith Barr*

> Be about your Father's business. There will always be plenty of other people occupied with the affairs of the world.
>
> *Frances J. Roberts*

> Man may dismiss compassion from his heart, but God will never.
>
> *William Cowper*

## Reflect

Do you schedule time for prayer and Bible study? Start with 10 minutes a day and see where God leads you. How has God been active in your life? Have you thanked Him? What is the greatest act of God's compassion recorded in the Bible? How does this affect your life? Ask God to send His Holy Spirit to increase your compassion for others.

## WEEK 28

Jesus, Savior, pilot me
Over life's tempestuous sea;
Unknown waves before me roll,
Hiding rock and treach'rous shoal.
Chart and compass come from Thee.
Jesus, Savior, pilot me.

# Money

We're struggling financially again.
There's not enough money to go around.
Some bills won't be paid, Lord.
I bring home a good salary—why can't
    we make ends meet?
Sure, we live comfortably,
    but we don't seem to save anything.
I feel guilty when I spend money on myself.
I want the best for my family,
    but it seems we miss out because
    we can't afford the luxuries.

Lord, remind me of the priceless
    treasure You've given us—Your love.
You dwell in our home and that
    overshadows everything else.
We love each other, and You love us.
That's much better than an IRA or a
    summer home on the lake.

Father, make us better caretakers of what
    You have given us.
Encourage us to share our riches with others.
    Amen.

# Calming the Storm

*The men ... asked, "What kind of man is this? Even the winds and the waves obey Him!" (Matthew 8:27)*

"Be still."

With these two words, You calmed the storm.
Your friends were in danger,
   scared for their lives.
They woke You, and You responded.

Storms scare me too.
I fear what could happen to me or
   my family.
What about sudden death or an accident?
I wonder how I'll react.

"You of little faith, why are you so afraid?"
Your words and actions teach me
   a valuable lesson.
I need to listen for Your voice and
   turn to You when storms approach.
I need to trust You to act in
   Your good time and in my
   best interests.
You amazed Your disciples, Lord,
   and You amaze me.
I stand in awe of the calm You give. Amen.

# Frustration

Trapped in a corner.
Not only do I dislike the prospects,
    but the outcome is out of my control.
I'm frustrated and a little angry.
My disposition stinks, and I'm pulling
    away from You.

I pray for patience but I really
    want out as soon as possible.
I want to move on to more
    productive activities.
Despite the futility of the moment, You are
    accomplishing Your will through this
    situation, Lord.
Show me Your desire and make me
    Your agent for change.

Lord, clue me in to Your plan for the future.
Give me a joyful and courageous heart to
    fulfill Your plans.
When it's finally time to move on, may I
    communicate love and concern as I do so.
Lord, strengthen my desire to
    serve You in all things. Amen.

# Week 28 Activities

**Themes:** Anxiety, difficulties, fear, frustration, money, security, wealth

**Old Testament Exploration:** Genesis 7:17–8:1; Psalm 16

**New Testament Exploration:** Matthew 6:24; Colossians 2:6–15

> A saint's life is in the hands of God as a bow and arrow in the hands of an archer. God is aiming at something the saint cannot see; he stretches and strains, and every now and again the saint says: "I cannot stand any more." But God does not heed; he goes on stretching until his purpose is in sight, then he lets fly. We are here for God's designs, not for our own.
>
> *Oswald Chambers*

> Christ made no promise that those who followed him in his plan of reestablishing life on its proper basic principles would enjoy a special immunity from pain and sorrow—nor did he himself experience such immunity. He did, however, promise enough joy and courage, enough love and confidence in God to enable those who went his way to do far more than survive.
>
> *J. B. Phillips*

## Reflect

What brings the most frustration to your life? Have you tried to handle it on your own? Ask God for help. Write three promises God makes in His Word to help you through your troubles on self-stick notes. Use them as reminders that God is always with you.

............................................

# W E E K   2 9

What magnificent changes God works in His followers. Consider the disciples. Under the Holy
Spirit's guidance, these mostly uneducated men
preached and baptized and spread God's Word.
But the greatest change God works in His followers takes place inside them. He took His former
enemies and, through the gift of faith, made
them His dearest children. Ask God to help you
witness to this change daily.

............................................

............................................

# Roses

Of all the plants and trees that
  grow in our yard, the
  roses are my favorites.
I adore their beauty and fragrance.

I see parallels between roses and my
  personal faith, Lord.
They both need a lot of attention, love,
  and care.

Beautiful roses don't just happen.
  They require the right combination of
  soil, moisture, and light.
  They must be nourished and pruned.
I must protect them from destructive
  elements, such as bugs or bike tires.
Beautiful roses take time.

My relationship with You, Father,
  requires the same careful attention.
Through Word and Sacrament, You
  strengthen me and prepare me to
  face the world's destructive elements.
Lord, challenge me to spend as much time
  cultivating my faith as I do my garden.
Make my life in You a thing of beauty just
  like the roses. Amen.

# A Quiet Disciple

*Joseph [of Arimathea] took the body, wrapped it in a
clean linen cloth, and placed it in his own new tomb.*
*(Matthew 27:59–60)*

Others who claimed Your friendship had
    forsaken You and fled.
Joseph of Arimathea came forward.
He provided not only the empty tomb, but
    he wrapped Your nail-pierced body.
What was his motivation?
You, Lord. You had touched his life.
And he had to respond.

Jesus, You have touched my life too.
You have changed me in ways I could
    never have imagined.
The power of Your Spirit motivates me to
    take on new challenges each day.
Your grace sustains me. I move forward boldly,
    knowing You forgive my shortcomings.
Like Joseph I act on Your love, seeking
    opportunities for service.

The reasons for Joseph's actions were
    kept private. He sought no glory.
Some may not even have known about his deed.

Lord, allow me to follow Joseph's example.
I often look for recognition.
I say that my acts of discipleship are to
    Your glory, but I often want to share
    the spotlight.
Give me satisfaction in serving You. Amen.

# Desert

It stretches for hundreds of miles.
Still hours from my destination,
    I will be traveling in this desert for
    the duration of my trip.
I feel alone as I travel.

To the side of the highway, I see a
    series of buttes.
Cactus and prairie grass grow from the
    parched ground.
Here, in the middle of an arid land,
    there is life.
Beauty flourishes where I had
    never seen it before.
How, in the midst of barrenness,
    can there be life?

I reflect on the times when I
    experienced spiritual drought.
In the middle of my arid spiritual wilderness,
    new life emerged.
You, Lord, brought the rains of
    renewal through Your Word and Sacrament.
Only in You do I receive new life.
Only in You does the earth find life.

As You restore my life with living water,
    please sustain this earth with
    life-sustaining rains.
Full of the miracles of Your creation,
    this land and my life bear
    testimony to Your love and power. Amen.

............................................

# Week 29 Activities

**Themes:** Beauty, discipleship, growth, life, love, nature, nurture, solitude

**Old Testament Exploration:** Genesis 1:1–2:1; Psalm 77

**New Testament Exploration:** Mark 10:17–31; Luke 14:25–35

> From morning to night keep Jesus in your heart, long for nothing, desire nothing, hope for nothing, but to have all that is within you changed into the spirit and temper of the Holy Jesus.
>
> *William Law*

> The beautiful can have but one source ... God.
>
> *Arthur Schopenhauer*

> The desert does not mean the absence of men, it means the presence of God.
>
> *Carlo Carretto*

## Reflect

What hobbies do you enjoy? Do you do them in solitude or with others? Why? How does God work through this leisure time to refresh you? Think about the most beautiful thing you've seen. Where did/does its beauty come from?

# WEEK 30

The family vacation—kids, wife, and a thousand suitcases crammed in the car. You drive 10 hours to stay in a noisy hotel next to the crowded amusement park. You're up early and run all day. Try scheduling a relaxing vacation this summer. Putter around the house. Make day trips around your hometown. Whatever you do, make time for daily renewal with God through devotions and prayer.

..........................................

# Summer

I've always been a summer person.
The warmth,
    the opportunity to be outside,
    even the summer heat,
    brings new energy to my cold-weary body.

I also enjoy the change in schedule
    summer offers.
The kids are out of school;
    I have fewer meetings and commitments.
The days seem to go on forever as
    sunlight extends well into the evening hours.

Father, make summer a time to get
    better acquainted with You.
May the more leisurely pace provide time for
    growth in our relationship.
I see the plants flourishing all around me,
    and I pray for that increase in my life.
Make this summer a fruitful time for me. Amen.

# Vacations

Why can't our vacations be like the ones in
the commercials?
Our time away seems more like a
series of hassles.
I return home feeling more tense than
when I left.

Vacations mean driving, and after
years of commuting, that's not fun.
Vacations mean constant whining and
bickering between the kids.
Vacations mean spending the first few days
learning to relax again.

Time off is important.
So is time spent together as a family.
We all need to kick back,
renew our bodies, minds, and spirits.
But why is it such a hassle?

Perhaps I've missed the point.
If I was seeking renewal in Your Word and
in prayer every day, maybe I wouldn't be
so tense.
My daily recreation would better
prepare me for the vacation.

Lord, help me realize vacations don't
have to be in exotic places
or cost a lot of money.
We vacation when we spend time together with
each other ... and with You. Amen.

..........................................

# Rest

*[Jesus said,] "Take My yoke upon you ... and you will find rest for your souls." (Matthew 11:29)*

I'm definitely weary tonight.
I'm exhausted from all the activity today.
If I ever needed to hear Your words
   of comfort, Jesus, it's tonight.

I read about taking on Your yoke.
Am I investing my time and energy in
   the right things?
How much of my daily activity serves me and
   my needs rather than meets
     Your desires for me?
I face tough decisions daily.
Am I using my talents and abilities to
   serve You?

Lord, help me focus on those tasks that
   will bring me closer to You.
Give me strength to fulfill my obligations
   to others.
Guide my activities so I will reach the
   end of hectic days with feelings of
     accomplishment and fulfillment in You.
Grant me rest for body and soul so I can
   start each day with a spirit
     refreshed by You. Amen.

............................................

# Week 30 Activities

**Themes:** Family, relaxation, renewal, rest, summer, vacation

**Old Testament Exploration:** Leviticus 25:1-7; Isaiah 40:28-31

**New Testament Exploration:** 2 Corinthians 9:6-15

> Recreation is not the highest kind of enjoyment; but in its time and place it is quite as proper as prayer.
>
> *S. Irenaeus Prime*

> Rest and motion, unrelieved and unchecked, are equally destructive.
>
> *Benjamin Nathan Cardozo*

## Reflect

How does God daily provide you with opportunities to renew your spirit? Do you ask God to bless your rest each night so you will wake up refreshed? What was your favorite vacation as a child? Why? Take the same trip (if possible) with your children and compare experiences.

## W E E K   3 1

Do you know the effect your daily witness has on others? You might if a friend joins your church or discusses God with you. But you touch untold numbers with God's love during your daily interactions. God can use even the briefest encounter to plant the seed of faith. Ask God to bless your witness so that even simple words and actions will speak volumes about His love in Christ.

# Yard Work

Father, You have blessed us with a
  beautiful home, but
  there's always yard work.
Don't get me wrong, I enjoy
  working in the yard,
Gardening provides recreation.
But it takes time, and
  the summer heat saps my energy.

Lord, I look at the yard and
  feel proud of the work I've done.
This little piece of property,
  humble as it is, is part of
  Your creation.
I'm but the caretaker.

Lord, keep me mindful of that.
Bring joy to my labor and make it
  a witness to my neighbors.
May they, through me, see Your love expressed,
Not just through my words and actions, but
  through the manicured lawn,
  the trimmed shrubs,
  and the fragrant roses. Amen.

# What Kind of Ground Am I?

*Still other seed fell on good soil, where it produced a crop—a hundred, sixty or thirty times what was sown. (Matthew 13:8)*

I'm glad You explained the
    parable of the sower, Jesus.
It's not that it's hard to understand.
Actually, it's quite easy.
But with such an important lesson,
    I'm glad You spelled things out
    so clearly.

But what kind of ground am I?
I've always claimed to be good ground—
    ground that should bear much fruit.
But do I ask You to fertilize me through
    daily contact with Your Word?
Do I celebrate Your presence in my life
    through worship and prayer?
Do I receive Your forgiveness and
    precious Body and Blood regularly?
Do I recognize the opportunities that
    You provide to witness my faith
    to others?

Jesus, these tough questions need
    honest answers.
Help me seek Your presence in my life through
    Word and Sacrament and
    grow in my faith.

May that growth be reflected in the abundant
    crop that seed of faith You planted
    produces in my life.

May the seed You sowed bear much fruit
    and spread
    to the lives of others through me. Amen.

······································

# My Easy Chair

It's been a long day, Lord, but now I can
    relax and get comfortable.
I can sit in my easy chair.
I can retreat and rest.

Tonight I write while a baseball game
    plays in the background.
Other nights I read, watch TV, dream, or
    catch a nap.
There's nowhere else in the house,
    maybe in my life,
    where I'm more at ease.

Jesus, I know You had Your
    private retreats.
You didn't have an easy chair,
    but You had the hills and perhaps
    a comfortable boulder to sit on.
There You were rejuvenated as You conversed
    with Your Father.
That's what prepared You
    for the work ahead.

Lord, please join me here.
You are part of my life,
    even when I'm retreating from
    the world.
My time here prepares me for the work
    out there.
Join me here and renew me, Lord.
Lord, thanks for this chair and for
    sharing it with me. Amen.

·············································

# Week 31 Activities

**Themes:** Maintenance, nurture, rest, retreat

**Old Testament Exploration:** Psalm 62:5–8; Isaiah 41:13–20

**New Testament Exploration:** Matthew 13:1–9, 18–23; 1 Corinthians 3:1–15

> The best things are nearest: breath in your nostrils, light in your eyes, flowers at your feet, duties at your hand, the path of God just before you. Then do not grasp at the stars, but do life's plain, common work as it comes.
>
> *Robert Louis Stevenson*

> God will never plant the seed of his life upon the soil of a hard, unbroken spirit. He will only plant that seed where the conviction of his Spirit has brought brokenness, where the soil has been watered with the tears of repentance as well as the tears of joy.
>
> *Alan Redpath*

## Reflect

What kind of ground are you? How does God tend you each day to keep the seed of faith alive? How does your life bear witness to this faith?

## W E E K   3 2

I doubt my faith would move a paperclip let alone a mountain. But that's the problem—our faith should be in God's ability to move mountains, not ours. On our own, we're nobodies. Faith makes us somebodies—God's dearly loved children. He sent Jesus to save you from your nothingness. Your faith is powerful enough to do anything because it's really God at work.

..........................................

# What I See and Believe

*"Are You the one who was to come, or should we expect someone else?"* (*Matthew 11:2*)

John the Baptist's disciples came to You
    on his behalf.
He wanted to know the truth.
Your response is a strong lesson.
"Go back and report to John what you
    hear and see."

This world is full of people
    looking for the truth.
They enter my life every day.
Sometimes their questions are direct,
    like that of John's disciples.
At other times they
    watch and listen for the subtle messages.
What knowledge am I relaying about
    You and Your relationship with me
    through my words and actions?

Jesus, through the power of the Holy Spirit,
    enable me to show and tell others what
    I know in my heart.
Make my life a powerful testimony to what
    You have done for me.
You are the one who was to come,
    and You have come into my life and
    changed me forever.
I was lost in sin until You rescued me.
That's Great News that has to be shared. Amen.

# Rain on the Picnic

The church picnic should be a
    joyous event, Lord.
I'm sure the organizers pictured a
    fun evening of food and fellowship.
I always look forward to the softball game:
    the parents versus the kids.
Then it rained. The picnic moved indoors.
Hot dogs, chips, and potato salad don't
    taste as good in a crowded gym.

We didn't really need the rain.
Some sun would have been nice today.
The kids could have run off some of
    their energy—outside.
Instead we're inside, and parents are
    learning a lesson in patience.

Lord, I trust Your good judgment.
The wind and rain are gifts from You.
Help me look for the good in this situation.
Remind me that good times aren't tied to
    good weather.
Fill me with the joy of Your presence. Amen.

........................................

# A Seed of Faith

*[Jesus said,] "The kingdom of heaven is like a mustard seed." (Matthew 13:31)*

I'm struggling in my relationship
   with You right now, Jesus.
I don't doubt my faith,
   but I'm having trouble putting it into action.
I'm having difficulty in my walk of
   discipleship, and that's
   hurting my self-confidence.
I feel like I'm drifting from You.

I don't doubt that You are still
   working in my life.
The seed of faith is still there.
Please cultivate the roots
   so it will grow stronger.
Help me return to the basics.
Bring me back to reliance on You.

I know from past experience that I'll go
   through times like this.
My sinful nature rises up, and I try to
   take control of my faith walk.
   I don't place my trust in You.
But knowing why I feel like this doesn't
   make things any easier.

That's why I appreciate the seed of
   faith You planted so long ago.
Thanks for faithful parents and teachers
   who instructed me.

Thanks for friends who support me
spiritually.
Thanks for staying with me and for
forgiving me for the times like this.

Jesus, send Your Holy Spirit to dwell
in my life.
I'm not looking for the faith to move
mountains, just the strength and power
to be Your servant where I am. Amen.

# Week 32 Activities

**Themes:** Actions, disappointments, faith, nurture, testimony

**Old Testament Exploration:** Genesis 22:1–18; Psalm 40:1–3

**New Testament Exploration:** Matthew 6:25–34; Romans 4:16–25

> What a man accomplishes depends on what he believes.
>
> *Anon.*

> Belief is truth held in the mind; faith is fire in the heart.
>
> *Joseph Fort Newton*

## Reflect

Do you believe Jesus is the one "who was to come"? Why? How do your words and actions reflect your belief? Do you frequently (daily) ask God to nourish the seed of faith He planted? Ask God to give you the strength to climb, even move, the mountains in your life.

Remember how you felt your first week at college? Recall your mom's description of your initial reactions to kindergarten. Separation can be traumatic. Sin separated you from God. But He reached out to you. He sent Jesus to lay down His life as the bridge across the void. God made you His child and promises never to be separated from you. Through faith, you will be with God in heaven.

# Leaving

I can see his figure in the rearview mirror,
    standing at the curb, waving.
I guess this is why his mother
    stayed home. Saying good-bye here is
    difficult.

Lord, I know we've been planning this for
    a long time.
It's what parenting is all about.
    You raise them to let them go.
We all know he's ready to leave.
I have no doubt about his talent or
    his maturity.
He's going to do well.

But it's difficult to let go.
I know he's going to face failures
    and disappointments.
He's going to struggle with some things
    and make some mistakes.

Lord, I place him into Your hands.
Watch over him and protect him.
Lift him up and forgive him when he falls.
I pray that my relationship with him
    will continue to grow while we're apart,
Just as I pray his relationship with
    You will grow. Amen.

# Mealtimes

Supper was a disaster tonight, Lord.
Mark spilled his milk.
    Peter was sulking because
    he had a bad day at school.
Then Katie decided that the applesauce looked
    better in her hair than on her plate.

I don't know how much more I can take.
    My stomach is in knots every evening.
At this pace, I'm going to keep the antacid
    manufacturers in business all by myself.
I remember when life was much simpler.
    It was so nice having dinner for two.
Now I dread mealtime.

Lord, give me the patience to make it through
    these times.
I know the day will come when I'll
    long for the noise of children.
Help me keep that in mind so I can
    enjoy these times.
Meanwhile, make me a model of Your love.
Keep me from blowing up. Give me the
    strength to care in the midst of chaos. Amen.

# Off to School

Lord, it's still scary to send
   our children to school each day.
I watched our son this morning as he walked
   down the drive.
My eyes followed him until he was
   out of sight.

He's 13 and becoming self-sufficient
   all too soon.
But that doesn't ease these daily misgivings
   I have as he takes off for school.
I'm aware of this world's dangers.
The threat of physical harm and the lure of
   temptation are ever present.

I must let him go.
Today he's miles away at school. Some day that
   distance might be greater.
Then, like now, I must entrust him to
   Your care.

Father, I think You know what that's like.
You let Your Son go once.
Unlike me, You had foreknowledge of what was
   ahead, the horrible suffering that would
   lead to the ultimate victory.
We rejoice that You let Him go.

Help me trust the plan You have for
  our children.
Allow me to let them go,
  knowing that in You, they
  will always be safe. Amen.

....................................

# Week 33 Activities

**Themes:** Acceptance, parenting, patience, school, trust

**Old Testament Exploration:** 1 Samuel 1:4–11, 20–28; Psalm 19

**New Testament Exploration:** Luke 2:41–52; Colossians 1:22–23

> The man who has been taught by the Holy Spirit will be a seer rather than a scholar. The difference is that the scholar sees and the seer sees through; and that is a mighty difference indeed.
>
> *A. W. Tozer*

> What greater work is there than training the mind and forming the habits of the young?
>
> *St. John Chrysostom*

## Reflect

What did you enjoy most about school? How did God bless you through your education? In your interaction with your children, how do you encourage their academic success? Ask God to be with your children and their teachers.

# W E E K   3 4

When you get hassled at work, picture Jesus (before His public ministry) working in His carpentry shop. Customers haggle over prices. Supplies run low. He longs for a vacation. It's comforting to think Jesus may have dealt with some of the same work issues you face. Jesus invites you to turn things over to Him. He understands your problems. He will guide you to solutions.

..............................................

........................................

# Labor Day

This is one holiday I've always
    struggled to find reasons to celebrate.
I've never been a union member.
    I earn my living sitting behind a desk.
I'm as white collar as they come.

But while the holiday may seem
    more important to the unions,
    I'm a laborer too.
I have a job.
I work hard every day.
Sure, I'm not on an assembly line somewhere,
    but sometimes I feel like I am.
This day is for me too.
It's a time to thank the
    people around me who work to
    make my life easier.
It's time to thank You, Lord,
    for the opportunity to work—
    whether in factory, field, or office.

Lord, help me see that I am
    more than an earthly laborer.
    I work within Your kingdom too.
You have given me specific gifts.
Through the power of Your Spirit,
    enable me to use them fully for
    the benefit of all Your people.
This is my prayer this day and always. Amen.

# Feeding the Hungry

*They all ate and were satisfied.* (*Matthew 15:37*)

I struggle to understand Your
    fantastic miracle of feeding the crowd.
I expect Your compassion on the people.
And the miracle of changing a
    small amount of food into enough to
    feed thousands of people
    reinforces Your awesome power.
It reminds me to have faith in Your good gifts.

But I struggle with understanding
    the need for food.
My family doesn't go hungry.
    We have a stocked refrigerator and pantry.
    We eat at fast-food places too often.
The picture of hungry people
    sitting on a hillside, or the
    reality of hunger all around us,
    is difficult to paint.

When You fed the crowd, the disciples
    turned to You as the supplier.
They provided the manpower to distribute
    the bread and fish.
Jesus, that's what we need today.
You still create and supply all we need.
As Your contemporary disciples, we need to do
    a better job of distributing
    what You have given us.
May it begin in our home. Amen.

# Bills

They greeted me as I opened the mailbox:
    the electric bill,
    the telephone bill,
    and the big bill from the orthodontist.
When will it end, Lord?
My paycheck is almost spent before it's
    even cashed.

I feel guilty that I owe money.
I feel cheated because there isn't enough
    left for the things I enjoy.
It seems like a never-ending cycle.
    Earn money; spend money.
And there's little to show for it.
But those bills represent someone else's
    income.
Whether directly or indirectly, those bills
    feed someone's family.

Lord, give me a positive spirit as I
    sort through and pay these bills.
Keep me mindful that You
    have paid off my greatest debt
    through the sacrifice of Your Son. Amen.

# Week 34 Activities

**Themes:** Debt, food, labor, money, responsibility, service, society

**Old Testament Exploration:** Exodus 16:1–36; Jeremiah 22:13–17

**New Testament Exploration:** Hebrews 13:1–8; James 2:1–13

> Take care of the pennies, the dollars will take care of themselves.
>
> *Anon.*

> Lord, turn the routines of work into celebrations of love.
>
> *Anon.*

> A Christian should always remember that the value of his good works is not based on their number and excellence, but on the love of God which prompts him to do these things.
>
> *St. John of the Cross*

## Reflect

Define your job. How does your job give you satisfaction? How does it challenge you? What opportunities does God give you on the job to witness for Him? If Jesus worked beside you, what would He see and hear? How does God provide for you through your job?

# WEEK 35

Water-skiing is pretty close to walking on water. As the boat pulls you, you glide across the surface. Until you start to worry and lose your concentration. Then you're bouncing across the waves, fearing for your life. As you walk across the spiritual water with Jesus, concentrate on Him. He won't steer you wrong. And if you start to lose control, He promises to steady you and keep you safe.

......................................................

# Decisions

This decision isn't clear-cut, but
    I must make it ... soon.
Whatever the outcome, people and
    feelings are involved.
That complicates things.
Part of life's process, decisions cause
    change and growth.
But decisions made in haste can result in
    hurt and loss.

Lord, this decision is important.
    Lives could change, it all hinges on
    my choice.
But in the middle of the upheaval,
    life will go on because
    You are still in charge, Lord.
Fortunately, our best and worst decisions
    are only temporal.
In days or years, the effects of
    our actions are often forgotten.

But Your decisions, Lord, affect lives
    forever.
You made the decision to
    sacrifice Your Son to save sinful humans.
    That was a permanent solution.
That decision changed the
    fate of humankind forever.

Lord, thanks for making such a
    bold decision. Amen.

# Walking

Lord, I enjoy my evening walks.
I remember younger days when I
   ran. Now I'm happy with a
   slower pace.

I enjoy the walk, but perhaps even more,
   I enjoy the talk with You.
I'm more aware of Your presence when
   I'm out walking.
The often-hectic pace of my life
   leaves few spare moments to share with You.
But when I'm walking, I can't do
   anything else.
That's what makes the time so precious.

Lord, thanks for my health and the
   strength to walk.
Thanks, too, for being a part of my life. Amen.

# Walking on Water

*Jesus went out to them, walking on the lake.*
*(Matthew 14:25)*

"Step outside your comfort zone."
That's something You call me to do
  as part of my walk of discipleship.
You call me to take risks, to step out
  in faith.
That was Your call to Peter, "Come."

Jesus, You made it look so easy.
"Come, Peter. Step out, Peter."
He tried, but the wind and the water
  intimidated him.
He sank. It was You who rescued him.

"Step out. Come to Me." That's Your call to
  me as well.
But like Peter, I find myself sinking more
  than walking.
My feeble attempts at boldly stepping out in
  faith usually end in failure.
That's why You took the walk first.
You not only walked on water but walked to
  the cross.

Jesus, go with me as I attempt to walk.
Keep calling to me so that, unlike Peter,
  I will keep my eyes on You at all times.
But Jesus, be ready. You and I know that,
  sooner or later, I'm going to need to
  be rescued again. Amen.

# Week 35 Activities

**Themes:** Decisions, guidance, prayer, rescue, trust

**Old Testament Exploration:** 1 Samuel 17:4–11, 32–51; Psalm 141

**New Testament Exploration:** Matthew 14:22–33; Hebrews 12:1–13

> God leads us step by step, from event to event. Only afterwards, as we look back over the way we have come and reconsider certain important moments in our lives in the light of all that has followed them, or when we survey the whole progress of our lives, do we experience the feeling of having been led without knowing it, the feeling that God has mysteriously guided us.
>
> *Paul Tournier*

> A single grateful thought raised to heaven is the most perfect prayer.
>
> *Gotthold Ephraim Lessing*

> Just walk on uninterruptedly and very quietly; if God makes you run, he will enlarge your heart.
>
> *St. Francis de Sales*

## Reflect

When do you spend time in prayer? Do you set time aside daily to talk with God? How is He involved in your decision making? How does God challenge

you to step out in faith? What gifts has God given you
in your faith walk?

# WEEK 36

Guilt wraps itself around your heart and sqeezes faith out. If you listen to guilt, it confirms your worst fear—you aren't worthy to be God's child. But Jesus *is* worthy. He took your punishment and made you sin-free in God's eyes. He filled your heart with the faith to say, "You are the Christ, the Son of the living God." Thank God for the faith to confess His name.

..................................................

# A Messy Room

It hit me like a ton of bricks when
    I walked into his room tonight.
I wasn't ready for the devastation.
Normally I can live with clutter, but tonight
    it was a combination of the mess
    and my mood.
I know I said something I shouldn't have.
    My temper got the best of me.
The bottom line is, he's promised to
    clean his room, but I hurt his feelings.

I should know by now that living with a
    messy room is really his business.
I'm also aware that there was probably a
    better way to handle the situation.
I know You will forgive me, Father, and
    he will too, in time.
But that's not the point.
My angry words and actions
    hurt people.

Father, one of the realities of
    living in a family
    is learning to accept others.
That means living with some annoying habits.
Keeping a messy room is something my son
    will probably outgrow.
Meanwhile, help me forgive his
    shortcomings,
Just as You forgive me. Amen.

# Guilt

I'm hurting. And to make matters worse,
    I brought this all on myself.
I made a mistake, and it's common knowledge.
Now I'm wallowing in guilt and self-pity.
Embarrassment keeps me from seeking support.
Instead of finding comfort in the
    fellowship of believers,
    I've cut myself off.

Father, I know people will welcome me back
    with a spirit of forgiveness.
That's the way Your family operates.
But it's difficult to walk into a group
    and ask for forgiveness.
I just want everything to
    return to normal without any
    acknowledgement of my mistakes.

But I know You want us to
    admit our mistakes and
    ask for forgiveness from those
    we've wronged and from You.
I need to hear the proclamation of
    forgiveness won for me by Jesus' death.
And I need the reminder that the
    victory over sin and the grave is
    mine through His resurrection.
Because of Jesus' saving work,
    I can celebrate the freedom
    forgiveness brings. Amen.

# A Confession

*Simon Peter answered, "You are the Christ, the Son of the living God." (Matthew 16:16)*

You asked the question, Jesus, and
Peter knew the answer,
"You are the Christ."
In many ways, that was the logical response.
Peter had experienced Your power and teaching
firsthand.
And Peter could confidently make the
statement,
surrounded by friends who had shared
his experience.
It was the right answer at the right time.

I'm not as bold as Peter.
I don't have his eyewitness
view to fall back on.
Instead of stating who You are, Lord,
I tend to look for excuses to
sit quietly, pretending the
situation isn't right.
I rationalize away the opportunities
You supply to proclaim Your name.
I mumble when I should shout;
I cower and cringe when I should
stand tall and proudly say,
"He's my Savior."

Jesus, enable me to make a bold confession.
When people ask, "Who do you think Jesus is?"

help me share my faith openly.
Guide me in those situations when I should
  share my faith with friends who are
  near to me but not close to You.
Especially make me a strong and
  confident witness in my own home. Amen.

# Week 36 Activities

**Themes:** Confession, forgiveness, guilt, regret, salvation, witness

**Old Testament Exploration:** 2 Samuel 12:7–17; Psalm 32:1–7; Psalm 38

**New Testament Exploration:** 1 John 1:5–2:6; Ephesians 2:1–10

> The purpose of being guilty is to bring us to Jesus. Once we are there, then its purpose is finished. If we continue to make ourselves guilty—to blame ourselves—then that is sin in itself.
>
> *Corrie ten Boom*

> In confession … we open our lives to healing, reconciling, restoring, uplifting grace of him who loves us in spite of what we are.
>
> *Louis Cassels*

## Reflect

What sins are weighing you down? Is there any sin that God cannot forgive? When you forgive someone, do you still remember the sin? Because of Jesus, God "remembers no more" our sin. He forgives us and does not condemn us (Romans 8:1). What does this mean for you?

# WEEK 37

*Scratch. Scratch-rub. Scratch.* The persistent scratching finally broke into my sleep. I let the cat in. He lept onto the bed and, with a contented sigh, snuggled next to my wife. God wants you to be persistent in your prayer life. He tells you to "pray continually." Constantly bring your needs and praises before Him. He promises to hear and answer your prayers—in His perfect time.

# The Responsibilities of Leadership

I didn't ask for this position.
Since no one else came forward,
   I was drafted.
Now here I am.
In preparation, I read Paul's list of
   leadership characteristics in his
   first letter to Timothy.
I don't think I measure up.
Considering the cost in time,
   I'm not sure I want to measure up.

Then I look at those whom I admire,
   the people who set the standards
   I want to follow, and
   they have some of the things Paul listed.
Despite their flaws, they strive to
   remain in control,
   respectable, and
   above reproach.

My Savior matches Paul's description.
In fact, He set the standards.
And Christ invites me to walk that walk,
   promising to forgive me when I fail.
Whether as a leader or not,
   Jesus has called me to follow.
Lord, please send Your Holy Spirit to
   guide my thoughts and actions. Amen.

# Loneliness

How can I be among so many people and
    feel alone?
Surrounded by familiar faces and
    friendly voices,
    I can't see or feel a thing.
An invisible wall holds back my
    feelings and emotions.
Alone with my fears and hurts,
    I'm slowly being destroyed.

I yearn for companionship and its many
    comforts.
    Won't someone listen to me?
I want to share my anxieties.
I want to be healed.
Then I hit the wall and the hurt grows.

Father, when will it end?
Where is Your mercy?
I know hope is out there.
But I feel so alone inside this
    self-made trap.
No, there's a response.
You are here—with me.
You're walking beside me.
There's hope.

Father, thank You for
    breaking down the wall
    between us.

Thanks for the gift of Your Son,
 who died and rose to bring
 us together.
Through the power of the Spirit,
 enable me to see You
 by my side—especially when I
 feel lonely. Amen.

# Persistence

*Jesus answered, "Woman, you have great faith! Your request is granted." (Matthew 15:28)*

Call it guts. Call it courage.
    Call it tenacity or fortitude.
Call it what You want, but I want it.
I'm tired of seeing myself as a quitter.

When I read of the Canaanite woman and her
    faith, I'm moved.
She not only trusted You but she
    challenged Your promises to her.
Her confidence in You paid off.
She won. Her daughter was healed.

I'm losing most of my faith battles, Jesus.
I think it's a lack of persistence on
    my part.
I start with great intentions but lose
    my enthusiasm along the way.
Somewhere along the line, my
    persistence fails me,
    and I feel defeated.
But the Canaanite woman held the key.
She came to You in total confidence.

Jesus, I want that kind of faith.
Through the power of Your Holy Spirit,
    strengthen me and make me
    confident of Your promises.
I'm tired of going through life as a loser.
    Make me a winner with You. Amen.

# Week 37 Activities

**Themes:** Companionship, confidence, determination, leadership, loneliness, perseverance

**Old Testament Exploration:** Genesis 18:16-33; 29:14-30

**New Testament Exploration:** 1 Peter 5:1-11; 1 Timothy 6:11-16

> To be a chief of people is to serve them.
>
> *Arabian proverb*

> By perseverance the snail reached the ark.
>
> *Arabian proverb*

## Reflect

List your qualifications for leadership. How do they measure against God's requirements in 1 Peter and 1 Timothy? How did Jesus show His leadership? (See John 13:2-17.) Are you confident in God's promises? Ask God for the confidence of Abraham and the persistence of Jacob.

# W E E K   3 8

Golf will always humble you. If it's not the water
on three, it's the sand on six or the oak tree on
fourteen. It's a lot like your spiritual life. You
think you're doing great only to be tripped up by
your pride. The *only* source of salvation is Jesus.
He played the perfect round, avoided all sin's
traps. Because of Him, the 18th fairway of your
life leads to heaven.

.........................................

# Fall

The season is changing.
Shorter days, cooler air, and the
    colorful transformation of leaves
    would seem to indicate that another
    summer is but a memory.
It's easy to become melancholy
    this time of year.
Increased pressures come with the fall schedule.
    There's less leisure time.
The passing of the season somehow reminds me
    that I am aging.
Another fall means one less summer to enjoy.

All seasons are a gift from You, Lord.
Their constant progression reminds me that
    You are still in control.
Fall means winter is coming, a
    rest for the land and a time of
    preparation for new growth.
Lord, help me take advantage of fall as
    an opportunity to see You at work.
Show me new ways to serve You and
    prepare for Your second coming. Amen.

# Golf

I've been a golfer for years.
I sometimes get frustrated because
  I haven't gotten better.
But I still enjoy the game.
I go to the golf course to relax.
No one can phone me or knock on my door.
And golf takes total concentration, so
  I can't think of much else and golf.

I take that back, Lord.
  I do think of You when I'm golfing.
The beauty of Your world astounds me.
I'm grateful that You have given us
  the game of golf to enjoy.
I know that some still view golf as a
  passion.
It becomes all-consuming and interferes with
  their relationship with You.
Lord, send Your Spirit to adjust my attitude.
Help me use my recreation time wisely
  and serve as an example to others.
Father, even when I'm on the golf course,
  I want to be Your disciple. Amen.

......................................

# Warning

*[Jesus said,] "For whoever exalts himself will be humbled, and whoever humbles himself will be exalted."* (*Matthew 23:12*)

Matthew 23 is a harsh condemnation, Jesus.
But the Pharisees and religious leaders of
    Your day deserved the rebuke.
Your message also applies to some of the
    leaders of Your church today.

It's a high calling to be a leader of
    Your church.
You call people to teach, preach, and serve
    within Your kingdom.
You condemned the Jewish church leaders
    because of their hypocritical attitude.
They didn't live according to the high
    standards they forced on others.
Their religion was all show.

Jesus, protect our leaders, and all Christians,
    from such a trap.
Through the power of Your Holy Spirit,
    help all of us grow in faith
    and wisdom each day.
Enable us to take regular, realistic
    looks at our thoughts and actions.
Help us catch the flaws and
    turn us back to You.
Forgive our sins of hypocrisy and conceit
    and create a right spirit within us. Amen.

................................................

# Week 38 Activities

**Themes:** Autumn, change, humility, hypocrisy, passions, pride, recreation

**Old Testament Exploration:** 2 Samuel 7:18–29; 2 Kings 5:1–14

**New Testament Exploration:** Matthew 23:1–12; Luke 18:9–14

> Each moment of the year has its own beauty … a picture which was never seen before and which shall never be seen again.
>
> *Ralph Waldo Emerson*

> Count not thyself better than others, lest perchance thou appear worse in the sight of God, who knoweth what is in man. Be not proud of thy good works, for God's judgments are of another sort than the judgments of man, and what pleaseth man is ofttimes displeasing to him.
>
> *Thomas à Kempis*

> I used to think that God's gifts were on shelves one above the other and that the taller we grew in Christian character the more easily we could reach them. I now find that God's gifts are on shelves one beneath the other and that it is not a question of growing taller but of stooping lower.
>
> *F. B. Meyer*

## Reflect

When has your pride caused you to fall? How does God work in your life to instill humility? How does Jesus' example in Matthew 23:1–12 help you in your struggles against false pride?

# WEEK 39

Sing the following song with the faith of a child:

Jesus loves me, this I know,
For the Bible tells me so.
Little ones to Him belong;
They are weak, but He is strong.

Yes, Jesus loves me,
Yes, Jesus loves me.
Yes, Jesus loves me,
The Bible tells me so.

..............................................

# Faith Like a Child

*[Jesus said,] "Unless you change and become like little children, you will never enter the kingdom of heaven." (Matthew 18:3)*

When Jesus brought the child into
    the middle of the disciples as an example,
    I remember the times I have put the
    emphasis on power and achieving
    personal greatness.
It's an easy trap to fall into.
Our world puts so much emphasis on
    success and control.
Humility is out.
Personal pride is definitely in.

Then I read these words, and I realize
    Your whole ministry exemplified
    humility and servanthood.
Even while You were surrounded by
    disciples who couldn't get earthly
    power off their minds,
You stayed true to Your Father's plan and
    went quietly and uncomplaining to
    the cross.

How many times have children been
    teachers when it comes to faith?
They're so trusting, but they also
    strive to grow and learn.
Jesus, through Your Holy Spirit,

give me a childlike faith.
As my trust in You grows, also
    increase my desire to be close to You.

You are an awesome God.
Keep my childlike curiosity about You alive.
Humble me with Your majesty and
    motivate me to grow spiritually. Amen.

# My Son's Birthday

It's Mark's birthday.
I can't tell if he's growing up or if
   I'm just growing older.
I remember the night he was born.
He's our second child, and we waited so long
   for him.
Mark exemplifies the maxim that
   no two people are ever the same.
That's how You planned it, Lord.

Now that he's approaching his teen years,
   new interests and challenges lie ahead.
We've been through the dating,
   the driving, and the high school thing
   once before, Lord.
I know You understand my prayer for patience.
I want the best for him.
I remember the dreams I had for him
   when he was born.
I presented him with a fire truck and a
   stuffed dog we named Sherman.
He still sleeps with Sherman every night—
   he and his dreams all cuddled together.

Mark has his own dreams now.
He will continue to determine his own
   direction in life.
His mother and I can provide the roots, but
   he will grow and leave home
   like his brother.
Lord, I place him into Your hands. Amen.

# The Soccer Game

Father, I enjoy watching our
   children compete in athletics.
You've given them the drive to excel
   beyond their abilities.
Today was a perfect example.
The game was close, but Mark was there,
   playing defense in his usual
   aggressive manner.
We scored and held on for the shutout.
   Victory is sweet.

The offense got the credit and the adoration.
The focus was on the winning goal, but I know
   it was a team effort.
I told Mark that on the way home.
It can be difficult to allow others to
   accept the credit when we know our support
   was vital.

Lord, You call us to be Your disciples,
   whether it's in the office or on the
   athletic field.
I want my children to enjoy giving their best,
   no matter who gets the credit.
   I want them to know the real credit goes
   to You.
Help me model this attitude for them. Amen.

........................................

# Week 39 Activities

**Themes:** Children, competition, family, fatherhood, faith, humility, sports

**Old Testament Exploration:** 1 Samuel 3:1–10

**New Testament Exploration:** Matthew 18:1–9; 1 Corinthians 2:1–10

> Humble thyself in all things.
>
> *Thomas à Kempis*

> Children learn what they observe.
>
> *Dorothy Knolte*

> It is not faith and works; it is not faith or works; it is faith that works.
>
> *Anon.*

## Reflect

What do your children learn from watching you? List five traits you hope they see in you. Ask God to help you live as a faith example for your children and others.

# WEEK 40

A nod of the head, a kind word, a thank-you, a smile. Are these part of your body language and vocabulary of respect? Many have forgotten the meaning of the word and neglected the actions that convey it. God wants His children to treat their neighbors with love and respect—for property, position, family ties, and beliefs. Ask Him to help you practice respect.

...........................................

........................................

# Prairie

I've heard some people complain how
   they dislike traveling through the
   Midwest.
They find the endless prairie boring.
But I lived on the plains for a long
   time, and I still find in them a
   simple beauty.
In comparison to the majestic
   mountains, the prairies might seem dull.
But I feel just as overwhelmed when I view
   the endless miles of waving
   grass and crops.

Prairies mean life.
Animals live amid the grasses.
And our country, even the world,
   bases its survival on our prairies and their
   crops of wheat,
   corn, and
   beans.

Lord, thanks for the prairie.
As I gaze off into the distance,
   keep me mindful of Your presence
   in my future.
Focus my heart on Your desire to
   care for me.
The prairie is but one example of
   Your generosity. Amen.

# Respect

*Show proper respect to everyone.* (*1 Peter 2:17*)

I've heard some upsetting conversations.
What really bothers me is the
    object of the criticism—our
    church's leaders.
Decisions are being questioned. I even hear
    some inquiries about integrity.
Friends are on both sides of the issue.
    Some are being hurt and
    others are doing the hurting.

Church leadership is a difficult issue.
Whether elected or appointed, these
    leaders serve as Your representatives.
Problems, when they arise, need to be
    addressed personally and expediently.
Everyone deserves respect, which includes
    a private meeting to discuss and
    solve a problem before airing it to the
    entire world.

Father, as Your faithful servant,
    help me act respectfully to those
    You have placed over me.
Bless those who lead Your kingdom
    here on earth.
Provide them with a full measure of
    Your Spirit that they may be both
    bold and strong.
May all our actions grow out of
    respect for You and Your Word. Amen.

# Matthew 18

*[Jesus said,] "If your brother sins against you, go and show him his fault, just between the two of you."* (*Matthew 18:15*)

Sometimes I think we hear about
   this verse too often.
Don't get me wrong, Lord, we need to hear it.
In our sinful world, retaliation and revenge
   are expected.
At the very least, we take the path of
   least resistance and avoid confrontation
   with the other party.
And it really grieves me that this happens
   within the community of believers—
   even with me.
But inevitably, someone offers up Matthew 18.

Don't get me wrong, Jesus.
Your lesson is important.
But when we remind each other, is it a
   statement of faith or an
   attempt to humiliate?

Jesus, make me part of the solution.
Change my heart and attitude toward
   those who wrong me and
   those who confront me with my sins.
Grant me a forgiving spirit in
   all my relationships.
Remind me to keep the discussion of
   wrongs private and to work for
   Your glory in all situations. Amen.

# Week 40 Activities

**Themes:** Admiration, beauty, creation, forgiveness, leadership, nature, relationships, respect

**Old Testament Exploration:** Psalm 8

**New Testament Exploration:** Matthew 18:15–17; 1 Peter 2:13–17

> If you have never heard the mountains singing, or seen the trees of the field clapping their hands, do not think because of that they don't. Ask God to open your ears so that you may hear it and your eyes so you may see it, because, though few men ever know it, they do, my friend, they do.
>
> *McCandlish Phillips*

> Let us be first to give a friendship sign, to nod first, smile first, speak first, and if such a thing is necessary—forgive first.
>
> *Anon.*

## Reflect

Name three people you respect. Why do you respect them? Thank God for their influence in your life. Think about how you respond to those who sin against you. Do you follow Christ's command in Matthew 18? How does God work through Christian confrontation to affect change? How does this private talk show respect for the other person?

# WEEK 41

Resentment divides. It builds walls of misunder-
standing and digs pits of anger that are hidden
under the cover of pride. The Pharisees and
church leaders resented Jesus' growing popularity.
Their resentment hardened their hearts to His
message. Ask God to destroy any resentment that
may block you from experiencing genuine Christian relationships with family and friends.

..........................................

# Being Late

I dislike tardiness.
People who are consistently late upset me.
Schedule delays frustrate me.
Now my flight has been delayed for an hour,
    and I'm tense and angry.
I'm going to be the one who's late.

Lord, You have given us the gift of time.
You ask us to be good stewards of all
    Your gifts, including time.
That's what motivates me to be punctual.
But Jesus, need dictated Your agenda
    more than the clock.

According to Your example, I should view
    disruptions in my agenda
    as opportunities, not inconveniences.
I could use my "waiting" time to seek
    new ways to serve You and
    share Your love. Amen.

# Traffic

Lord, I'm not going anywhere.
I'm not referring to my career or my
    professional status.
I'm talking about the traffic.
I was already running late, I'll
    admit that.
I just hadn't anticipated this.
I hope it's only an overheated car and not a
    bad accident.

Highways are great.
We can travel safely for miles at
    high speeds.
We can also sit on them, occasionally
    creeping forward a few feet.
Is there a lesson for me here, Lord?

Maybe it's patience? Teach me to wait on You,
    even when the interstate is jammed.
Maybe it's trust? Remind me Your will
    will be done,
    even if it's not on my schedule.
Maybe it's compassion? Encourage me to pray
    for the person whose car is stalled or for
    those involved in the wreck.

All time is Your time, even when I'm
    standing still.
Help me relax and celebrate
    Your presence now. Amen.

# Guard Me from Resentment

*[Jesus said,] "So the last will be first, and the first will be last." (Matthew 20:16)*

The story of the vineyard workers
    doesn't seem fair.
Even today society struggles with
    the maxim presented.
We expect to receive what we earn.
If someone does less than us, we
    expect to receive more money,
    praise, or whatever the reward is
    measured in.
We live by this standard.
When it isn't followed, we all
    become irritable.

It's happening now at work.
I'm shouldering more responsibility,
    and trying to maintain a good attitude,
    but I'm not getting anything more
    in return.
In fact, others aren't carrying their weight,
    and they're receiving credit for
    things they haven't done.

I even face this situation at home.
Like when Mark is the only one who
    helps with the yard work.
Then he expects to get an extra big allowance
    because he did more work.
And everyone else says it's
    not fair for him to get more money

unless they do too.
Then I see the resentment in
my own reactions to how the
rewards of others compare to mine.
Sometimes I become bitter and unhappy.

Lord, it shouldn't be this way.
Touch every aspect of my life with
Your forgiveness.
Here's the perfect example of getting
what we don't deserve.
May that insight produce seeds of
love and joy in my life and
wash away any feelings of resentment. Amen.

........................................

# Week 41 Activities

**Themes:** Contentment, opportunity, patience, resentment, responsibility, stewardship, time

**Old Testament Exploration:** Psalm 31:14–15a; Ecclesiastes 3:9–17

**New Testament Exploration:** Matthew 20:1–16

> Use everything as if it belongs to God. It does. You are his steward.
>
> *Anon.*

> If you hug to yourself any resentment against anybody else, you destroy the bridge by which God would come to you.
>
> *Peter Marshall*

> Take time, strangle some other interests, and make time to realize that the center of power in your life is the Lord Jesus Christ.
>
> *Oswald Chambers*

## Reflect

How did you spend your time today? Did you give any back to God in Bible study or prayer? How is God's Holy Spirit leading you to make wise use of your time, talents, and treasures? How does God guard you from resentment in work or family life?

# W E E K   4 2

"It's not my fault!" Do you use that excuse? Why? Be honest—you don't want to take the fall. God doesn't accept passing the blame. Look at His response to Adam's attempt to accuse Eve. You sin. I sin. We can't dodge it. But Jesus—who *is* without fault—took the fall for us and gives us His perfection! Ask God to guide your actions so they will reveal this incredible gift to others.

..................................................

# The Bug

I'm sick!
Not sick enough to go to bed,
    just sick enough not to feel well.
So I struggle on, running a mild fever and
    aching all over.

Why now, Lord?
It's such a busy time, I can't
    afford not to be at my best.
Deadlines need to be met, and I need to
    finish that big project.
I guess I've been working harder than usual.
And I probably haven't been watching my
    diet and getting the proper rest.
Sometimes You do what You have
    to, Lord, to get my attention.

Lord, heal me. Help me feel better.
Help me slow down and get some rest.
Relieve some of the tension and anxiety so
    I could even take a day off.
Lord, be with me as I recover from this bug.
Quickly restore me to joyous service to You.
    Amen.

························································

# Fast Food

Lord, I can't handle another
　　burger and fries.
My body doesn't need the cholesterol.
And somehow it doesn't taste good anymore.
But I don't want to disappoint the kids.
And my wife can take it easy when she
　　doesn't have to cook and clean up.
And we get time to talk.

I wonder what we're doing to
　　our bodies.
I wonder what the term *fast food* says about
　　our lifestyle.

Jesus, You didn't have fast food.
You took time to enjoy food and
　　fellowship with those You loved.
I think Your meals were more a celebration
　　than a routine.
Lord, help us remember that You want to
　　join us wherever we eat.
Your presence makes the meal special.
Bless our burgers and fries,
　　tacos, pizza, and
　　garden salad with low-cal dressing. Amen.

# Healing

*Jesus reached out His hand and touched the man. "I am willing," He said. "Be clean!" (Matthew 8:3)*

Jesus, You have boundless compassion
   and unlimited power.
A man came to You with leprosy.
Cast out by his friends and family,
   he was without hope.
You saw his faith, touched him, and
   said, "Be clean!"

Acts of healing, of compassion, of love fill Your
   life story.
But where are the miracles
   today?
There are miraculous recoveries from cancer,
   dramatic organ transplants,
     but somehow they don't compare.
You truly give all
   good gifts, but why don't doctors
   and surgeons praise You for their expertise?
They claim the glory and honor due to You.
Your miracles become their daily work.
"Jesus, where are the miracles?" I ask again.
And then You reply, "Look at what

I've done for you.
Your life was broken,
    and I healed it.
You sinned and needed forgiveness,
    and I covered it."

Thanks, Lord, for Your
    miraculous healing in my life. Amen.

# Week 42 Activities

**Themes:** Healing, miracles, sickness

**Old Testament Exploration:** 2 Kings 4:8–37

**New Testament Exploration:** Matthew 8:1–4; James 5:13–20

> When God wants to move a mountain, he does not take a bar of iron, but he takes a little worm. The fact is, we have too much strength. We are not weak enough. It is not our strength that we want. One drop of God's strength is worth more than all the world.
>
> *Dwight Lyman Moody*

> Make sickness itself a prayer.
>
> *St. Francis de Sales*

## Reflect

How do you handle illness? How do you handle someone else's illness? How does God supply you with the strength and healing you need? Thank God for His love and care.

Work evaluations have replaced report cards in your life. As you're measured against your peers, will you be judged worthy of a promotion or a raise? There's one evaluation you never have to worry about—God's. Instead of looking at your failures, God looks at Jesus' perfect performance. Thank God for the glowing review you receive because of Jesus' life, death, and resurrection.

# Family Responsibilities

*If anyone does not provide for his relatives, and espe-
cially for his immediate family, he has denied the
faith and is worse than an unbeliever. (1 Timothy
5:8)*

My family is a gift from You, Lord.
And that gift isn't just my wife and children,
    it includes my extended family.
I owe so much to my parents, grandparents,
    and siblings.
They have made me what I am.

Lord, prevent me from ever taking the
    gift of family for granted.
Help me show love and appreciation during
    those times we are apart, and especially
    when we're together.

Make my entire family's welfare be of
    constant interest.
In my own home, help me develop an
    atmosphere of mutual respect and love
    that will stand the tests of time and distance.
May the priceless moments we share now
    become the memories that sustain later.

Father, You set the example of trust and love
    in Your relationship with Your Son.
    Help me follow it in my family life. Amen.

# Report Cards

I could tell something was up when I
   picked them up at school.
The whole student body seemed sedated.
I sensed an uneasy anticipation, like
   something dreadful was about to occur.
Our conversation on the trip home revealed
   the reason for the somber mood.
"We got our report cards today, Dad."

Actually they did quite well, Father.
They were up in some subjects and down
   a little in others.
All in all, it was pretty much as expected.
And I give thanks for the gifts, abilities, and
   unique traits You have given each one.

Lord, it's easy to attach success in life to a
   report card.
But it's an arbitrary judgment.
Thankfully, You don't judge us that way.
With salvation in Your Son, competence doesn't
   matter.

Lord, help us teach our kids in a way that
   affirms them and focuses on You as
   the Giver of all gifts.
Help us celebrate the uniqueness You have
   created in each of us. Amen.

# A Voice on the Phone

Lord, tonight I'm hundreds of miles
    from home.
My children are mere voices on the phone.
It's hard to express intimacy
    without touch.
Yet I know that right now,
    the phone is the best I can do.

They share the events in their lives.
    Katie has a difficult assignment in math;
    the coach complimented Mark on his
    intensity during soccer practice.
I wish I was there to aid in the struggles
    and join in the celebrations.
The reality is that I'm here and
    they are there.

Lord, enable me to express all my love and
    affection through words tonight.
    Words are all I have.
May they sense my love and compassion,
    even though
    they can't experience my touch.

Father, You are here, as well,
    even though there's no
    physical touch.
Your presence in my life is constant.
Help me model this in my relationship with
    my children.
Help me to be a loving father, even though
    distance separates us. Amen.

........................................

# Week 43 Activities

**Themes:** Education, family, grades, love, relationships, responsibility

**Old Testament Exploration:** Deuteronomy 11:18–21

**New Testament Exploration:** 1 Timothy 3:1–13

> Do today's duty ... and do not weaken and distract yourself by looking forward to things that you cannot see and could not understand if you saw them.
>
> *Charles Kingsley*

> I believe the family was established long before the church, and my duty is to my family first. I am not to neglect my family.
>
> *Dwight Lyman Moody*

> What does love look like? It has hands to help others. It has feet to hasten to the poor and needy. It has eyes to see misery and want. It has ears to hear the sighs and sorrows of men. That is what love looks like.
>
> *St. Augustine*

## Reflect

List the blessings God gives you to support yourself or your family. What needs do you or your family have? Have you brought these needs to God? What steps is God leading you to take to meet these needs?

How does your involvement in work or even church activities cause you to neglect your family? How do you handle separation from your family? While Jesus was here on earth, how did He keep in touch with His Father?

# WEEK 44

To whom or to what are you loyal? Probably to someone or something that you believe in, that will also stand by you. Are you loyal to God? Do you defend His name? Do you support His positions? Are you willing to give up everything, even your life, for Him? Even in your sin, God loyally stood by you and sent Jesus to give His life for you. Ask God to strengthen your loyalty to Him.

..................................................

# Worship

There seems to be a lot of
    discussion about worship styles, Lord.
What's proper, what's not,
    who can lead, who can sing,
    who can pray, what liturgy,
    what songs.
There must have been great variety in
    worship experiences in the early church.
There were probably vast differences between
    the worship of the apostles in Jerusalem
    and that of new believers in Ephesus.
    And what about Roman worship in the
    catacombs?
How can you sing hymns without an organ?

Lord, in the disagreement over style,
    aren't we losing sight of
    Your message?
You want all people to be saved
    and come to the knowledge of the Gospel.
You want sincere and honest prayers.
You want us to seek Your will.

Father, help me worship You with my
    whole self.
Make me both regular and sincere in
    my worship.
I don't want to just mouth
    words of praise.

I want to celebrate Your presence.
Grant me the privilege of seeing
    many different styles of worship—
    a bowed head and folded hands,
    children singing off-key but from the heart,
    drums and dance,
    symphonies, choirs, a single voice,
    a silent thought of praise. Amen.

# Loyalty

*[Jesus said,] "Give to Caesar what is Caesar's, and to God what is God's." (Matthew 22:21)*

Jesus, where should my real loyalty be?
Some government leaders couldn't care less
    about Your kingdom.
And it seems like they don't have
    America's best interests in mind either.

Loyalty is lacking at work too.
Some employees display a disgruntled attitude.
Others break out in open rebellion.
Either way, their actions work against
    the common good.
I admit I agree with their causes at times.
So Jesus, who deserves my loyalty?

Your answer seems to imply divided loyalty.
It's okay to support evil
    management and government,
    just make sure God gets what's His.
But that's not Your intent.
God is in charge of all things,
    including governments and bosses.
His chosen leaders deserve my respect and
    loyalty as long as they don't ask
    me to go against what You command.
Serve government, serve the faith community,
    serve my family, but do it in Jesus' name,
    who out of loyalty gave
    His life for me. Amen.

..........................................

# Reformation Day

In the eyes of the world,
    this day gets overlooked.
Halloween, and its emphasis on
    witches and goblins, overshadows the
    wonderful spiritual significance
    this day has for me.
It's hard to get children excited about
    Martin Luther and faith by grace
    when there's free candy available.

Luther's emphasis on Your grace
    changed the visible church forever.
People not only rediscovered Your Word, but
    the loving message of salvation
    contained in it.
Lord, I thank You every day for the
    free gift of salvation that
    I have through Christ.
You have clothed me—a sinner—in Christ.
Through Your Spirit, You have made me a
    new creature and have brought me
    into Your family through Baptism.

Lord, through my celebration of
    Reformation Day, may others
    see its meaning in my life.
May we all celebrate the legacy we have
    as Your forgiven people. Amen.

..........................................

# Week 44 Activities

**Themes:** Celebration, faith, government, loyalty, praise, reformation, salvation, worship

**Old Testament Exploration:** Exodus 20:8–11; Psalm 100

**New Testament Exploration:** John 4:19–26; Romans 3:21–28

> A person may go to heaven without health, without riches, without honors, without learning, without friends; but he can never go there without Christ.
>
> *John Dyer*
>
> God governs the world, and we have only to do our duty wisely and leave the issue to him.
>
> *John Jay*
>
> Worship requires only a man and God.
>
> *Anon.*

## Reflect

List the reasons you enjoy worship. Now think about why you don't enjoy worship. Ask God to help you work on the *important* issues. How does knowing God is in control affect your citizenship decisions? What does Jesus' statement in Matthew 22:21 mean to you? How do you celebrate your faith? Ask God to bless your celebration and your witness.

# W E E K   4 5

God is visible all around you. His beauty and power is made manifest in His creation. His love can be seen in the interactions of His people. His concern can be felt in the tender care a parent gives a child. God reaches out to His world through the talents He has given to you. He has made you His witness to those around you. Ask Him to strengthen and bless you for your tasks.

..........................................

# All Saints' Day

On All Saints' Day, I can't help
    thinking of Aunt Phyllis.
She was more than my aunt.
She was my godmother,
    my first-grade Sunday school teacher,
    and my forever friend.
Aunt Phyllis took me to my first movie
    and taught me to play pinochle.
Most important, she was a model of
    discipleship.
She corrected me when I was
    out of line and always
    practiced what she preached.
To me, she always meant love.

That's what makes this day special.
Each of us, on a daily basis,
    rubs shoulders with people who
    represent You, Lord, in our lives.
Through them, Your message of
    love, grace, and salvation,
    takes on real meaning.

Thanks for all the saints, Father.
They enriched our lives and
    served, defended, and extended
    Your kingdom.
Through the power of Your Spirit,
    enable me to walk proudly in
    their path as Your
    contemporary saint and disciple. Amen.

# Anointing with Gifts

*While Jesus was in Bethany ... a woman came to Him with an alabaster jar of very expensive perfume, which she poured on His head.* (Matthew 26:6–7)

Jesus, had I been present,
  I would have stood with Your disciples.
I can't help but think of the price tag;
  the money could have been better used.
I realize it was her way of responding to
  Your love, but isn't there a better way?

The money spent on lavish churches and their
  furnishings has always bothered me.
You are a great and magnificent God,
  deserving of the praise we offer,
  but is spending money the way to honor You?
Wouldn't it be better to serve You through
  the use of our gifts and talents?
Isn't Your kingdom better served when people
  are fed and the Gospel shared?
Jesus, didn't You commission us to build
  Your kingdom and not opulent buildings?

Jesus, begin with me. Through Your Spirit,
  change my life.
Make me a good steward of all the gifts You
  give me, especially my time and talents.
May my life be an outpouring of abundant
  blessings, precious ointment to be used
  to honor You and build Your church. Amen.

........................................

# Talents

*Everyone who has will be given more, and he will have an abundance. (Matthew 25:29)*

Jesus, I'm struggling with depression.
I've been passed over again.
They picked someone else for the position.
My evaluation stated that while I have specific
    skills, I'm not what they're looking for.
End result: I'm stuck where I am.

Father, You have given me many talents,
    but I'm still lacking something.
Those talents I do have seem
    ordinary when compared to others.
In most people's eyes, I'm a jack-of-all-trades
    and master of none.

I feel most closely aligned with
    the third servant in
    Jesus' parable of the talents.
I want to bury my talents and be left alone.
I'm quite satisfied with a low-risk,
    status-quo approach.
Jesus, You don't want it this way.
You desire the best.
Your sacrifice on Calvary demands that.

Restore excitement and motivation to my
    life.
Heal me from the wounds I've suffered.
Enable me to be realistic in evaluating my
    talents, then to use the ones that
    will benefit the church. Amen.

# Week 45 Activities

**Themes:** Offerings, saints, stewardship, talent, worship

**Old Testament Exploration:** Genesis 4:2–5; Micah 6:6–8

**New Testament Exploration:** Matthew 25:14–30; Revelation 21:1–4

A saint is one the light shines through.

*Anon.*

God creates out of nothing—wonderful, you say; yes, to be sure, but he does what is still more wonderful. He makes saints out of sinners.

*Sören Kierkegaard*

There is no portion of our time that is our time, and the rest God's; there is no portion of money that is our money, and the rest God's money. It is all his; he made it all, gives it all, and he has simply trusted it to us for his service. A servant has two purses, the master's and his own, but we have only one.

*Adolphe Monod*

## Reflect

Who has God placed in your life as an "Aunt Phyllis"? How does this person model God's love and his or her faith for you? Write or call and tell this person how important he or she is to your faith life. What gifts do you offer God? Are they your best or just what you have "laying around"? How does good stewardship of your time, talents, and treasures make a pleasing offering to God? Ask God to send His Spirit to help you in your stewardship life.

# W E E K  4 6

How do you know you love someone? Is it the smile on your face or the beating of your heart? Is it the sense of completeness that person brings? The love God gives you for your wife or kids or family binds you together in Him. It's a shared experience of respect, trust, hope, joy, fulfillment, and forgiveness. Only a perfectly loving God would give His creatures the gift of love.

..............................................

# Dinner Out

Lord, I've been looking forward to this
    all week.
It's a chance to relax and spend time with
    my wife.
The food and atmosphere are secondary.

Some might consider this
    poor stewardship.
It costs more to eat here than to eat
    at home.
But the attention and service allows us to
    focus on each other.
With our hectic schedules, that's
    reason enough to celebrate.

Lord, thank You for dinners out.
Grace us with Your presence,
    just as You do when we eat at home.
Bless our conversation,
    just as You do the food.
May our bodies be nourished and our spirits
    renewed for the days ahead. Amen.

# A Wedding

Jon and Sharon's son got married last night.
They're a neat couple, and the wedding was
   beautiful.
I still get sentimental at weddings.
There's something about seeing two people
   who are so much in love.

I don't view marriage as passè
It's a lifelong commitment.
Father, I believe You've given us marriage as
   a sign of Your love for us.
Just as Your love is constant and unchanging, so
   should our love be for each other,
   especially within the bonds of marriage.

Lord, bless our home.
It's not always perfect; we have our
   struggles.
But Your Holy Spirit is part of our family.
   And because of Your presence, there's
   an abundant supply of love.
Help me cultivate that love
   and share it with my wife. Amen.

# Going Home

Father, it's good to be home.
It's great to see familiar faces
   and to taste Mom's cooking.
The memories of this house
   and this neighborhood
   come flooding back.

I remember growing up here—
   the friends,
   the things we did together,
   fishing in the river,
   bike rides,
   and marathon Monopoly games.

Past events have made me what I am.
I remember the past, both victories
   and defeats, but I can't allow
   the past to control my future.

Father, thanks for the past. Bless the future.
Thank You for Your presence in the past,
   in the here and now, and in my future. Amen.

# Week 46 Activities

**Themes:** Commitment, family, love, marriage, roots, weddings

**Old Testament Exploration:** Genesis 2:24; Proverbs 18:22

**New Testament Exploration:** Matthew 19:4–6

> Marriage has in it less of beauty, but more of safety, than the single life; it has more care, but less danger; it is more merry, and more sad; it is fuller of sorrows, and fuller of joys; it lies under more burdens, but is supported by all the strengths of love, and charity, and those burdens are delightful.
>
> *Jeremy Taylor*

> Nothing is sweeter than love, nothing stronger, nothing higher, nothing wider, nothing more pleasant, nothing fuller or better in heaven or on earth. ... Though wearied, it is not tired; though pressed, it is not straitened; though alarmed, it is not confounded; but as a lively flame and burning torch, it forces its way upwards and passes securely through all.
>
> *Thomas à Kempis*

> God made marriage an indissoluble contract; the world today has made it a scrap of paper to be torn up at the whim of the participants.
>
> *Cardinal George William Mundelein*

## Reflect

When was your last date? Why was the date special? Ask God to bless your time alone with your wife. List five things that make marriage successful. What was number 1 on your list? Why? Is it a part of your relationship? Ask God to be the tie that binds you and your wife together. Why is your extended family so important to you? How did God work through your parents and siblings to bring you to this point in your life? Thank them and Him for their love and support.

Grandparents and parents recount times of need and plenty, the wealth of changes they've experienced, the advent of the technology revolution. God works through science and industry to help His human creatures. Thank Him for the speed and ease of modern transportation, the "togetherness" experienced through modern communication, and the quality of life you enjoy from modern conveniences.

# 30,000 Feet above It All

Here I am cruising in this capsule.
The airline's mistake put me in this
    window seat.
My long legs miss the extra aisle legroom,
    but it's a clear day so
    I get an incredible view.

What marvelous technology we have that allows
    airplanes to fly.
More marvelous, Lord, is the
    magnificent world You have created.
Whether majestic mountains or scenic lakes
    or Texas prairie, the beauty overwhelms.

We fly over farms and towns and cities.
Those are Your people, Father, even if
    they don't know You personally.
Those people have hurts and needs and joys.

Lord, the world is in Your hands.
    It's fragile and needs lots of care.
The people of the world are in
    Your hands also.
Watch over us and protect us.
And if some don't know the
    Good News of salvation through
    Your Son, send messengers into
    their lives to share the Gospel.

Lord, the whole perspective changes when
    you fly at 30,000 feet. Amen.

......................................

# Cars

The automobile—what a great invention!
  But what a strain to maintain.
Yes, my car's in the shop again.
It's just maintenance stuff, but I'm being
  "nickeled and dimed" to death.

We need transportation.
It's not just for commuting. A car
  represents the freedom to travel,
  to do things as a family.
A lot of memories ride on those four wheels.

There are many conveniences that
  You have provided for our
  comfort and freedom.
Help us not to take them for granted.
Remind us that all blessings come with
  responsibilities.
We should use everything to Your glory.
Even our cars are gifts to be used
  in service to You.

You've given us the greatest gift—
  Your Son.
The rest is just "frosting on the cake." Amen.

# Television

You have given us a real gift in
    television, Lord.
Through it, we see things we would
    never otherwise see.
It not only informs us, it
    entertains us.

But today I came home to find my daughter
    staring at the TV.
Sure she was watching Captain Crazy's
    Cartoon Festival, but I'm convinced
    her mind was in a trance.

Lord, keep us from using the TV as a
    baby-sitter.
Help us control this tool You have given us.
Give us wisdom to know when to turn it on and
    when to turn it off.
Help us use it to bring us together,
    not to build walls between us.

May the TV help us learn about the
    needs of other people in Your world.
May it help us discover new ways to
    serve You.
May it never expose us or our children to
    values that conflict with
    Your desires for us.

Lord, if You gave us TV, it must be good.
Help us find that good in it. Amen.

........................................

# Week 47 Activities

**Themes:** Blessing, priorities, thanksgiving

**Old Testament Exploration:** Psalm 106:1–5; Joel 2:21–26

**New Testament Exploration:** 1 Timothy 6:17

> Our intellect and other gifts have been given to be used for God's greater glory, but sometimes they become the very god for us. ... Even God cannot fill what is full.
>
> *Mother Teresa*

> Remember the wonderful blessings that come to you each day from the hands of a generous and gracious God, and forget the irritations that would detract from your happiness.
>
> *William Arthur Ward*

## Reflect

What modern conveniences are you most thankful for? When do they become temptations? How are they blessings from God?

Football. Turkey. Stomachaches. Is this Thanksgiving? Your wife has probably asked you that question. Surprise your wife with a card and a note that lists the reasons you thank God for her. Include the goofy ones like "You make corn because I hate peas." Include some of the reasons in your Thanksgiving table prayer. Then remember to thank God each day for the woman you married.

..........................................

# Thanks

Mashed potatoes, turkey and dressing,
   desserts as far as the eye can see.
It's a spread worthy of this
   stuff-'em-till-they-drop-in-front-of-the-TV
   holiday.
For a day that started with such a
   noble purpose, we've certainly
   managed to pervert it.

Lord, I'm confronted by the fact that
   Thanksgiving no longer has much to do
   with giving thanks.
It focuses on gluttony and sports and
   only momentarily on You.
For some people, the question may even be,
   "Why say thank You?"—
   I worked hard for all of this.
It's so easy to overlook You in
   the good times, Lord.

But You never forget us.
You send the rain on the just and the unjust,
   whether we say thanks or not.
Our tables overflow and bank accounts bulge
   whether we remember You or not.
What a great God You are.

And nowhere is Your greatness more apparent
   than on the cross.
You sent Your only Son to save us—
   a gift given freely with no
   expectation of repayment.

Nor can we repay the great price—and
our thank Yous seem insignificant.

But thank You, Lord, for the
bounty on our table,
for family and friends,
for possessions and jobs,
and for the extras too numerous to count.
A special thank You for the gift I treasure most,
my salvation.
Words cannot express my gratitude. Amen.

# What's Right?

*Everything God created is good.* (1 Timothy 4:4)

Sometimes I wonder what's right,
     and what's wrong?
At times I have trouble deciding.
It's almost like a game.
How do I know what's right in a
          particular situation?
     With which friends can I drink alcohol and
     who are the ones who don't eat meat?

Lifestyles, eating habits, musical preferences,
     there are so many ambivalent areas.
I don't crusade for any cause.
I want to enjoy life and get along with others.
Is that possible?

People seem to have drawn the line on
     so many issues.
I rebel when they force their opinions on me.
If everything You made is good, where did
     we go wrong?
Sin. From the time of Adam and Eve,
     sin has caused divisions on earth and
     between You and Your created people.
But You sent Jesus to heal that division, Father.
You have called me to a life of service to You.

Father, make me a vehicle for peace and unity.
May I do all things to Your glory.
Make my "cause" the extension
     of Your kingdom to all people. Amen.

# Popcorn

Lord, You have a way of giving us simple
    gifts that make even ordinary times
    special.
Popcorn is one of those gifts.
I watch through the microwave door as the
    kernels explode inside the bag.

Popcorn plays a role in our family events.
We nibble on it and laugh
    as we play a game together.
We munch quietly as we watch a video.
A shared bag of popcorn even brings a
    sense of intimacy to late-night discussions.

Popcorn is inexpensive and easy to prepare.
But You thought to create it.

I thank You for the gift of popcorn ...
    and for the most important gift—
    Your Son.
Jesus' presence makes all times and events
    special. Amen.

# Week 48 Activities

**Theme:** Thanksgiving

**Old Testament Exploration:** Exodus 15:1–21; Psalm 118

**New Testament Exploration:** Matthew 15:35–37; Luke 17:11–19

> Pride slays thanksgiving, but an humble mind is the soil out of which thanks naturally grows. A proud man is seldom a grateful man, he never thinks he gets as much as he deserves.
>
> *Henry Ward Beecher*

> Thanksgiving was never meant to be shut up in a single day.
>
> *Robert Caspar Lintner*

## Reflect

What three things are you most thankful for? Why? Do you take time each day to *thank* God for His blessings, big and small? Do you *thank* God for the trials that bring you closer to Him? What part of your life is like popcorn—a simple gift?

# WEEK 49

You flush the radiator, put on snow tires, check
the battery, and fill the fluids, carefully winteriz-
ing your car. Are you as careful in your prepara-
tions for Jesus' second coming? Do you read and
study God's Word regularly? Do you faithfully
attend worship? Do you frequent the Lord's
Table? Do you talk with God daily? Ask Him to
make this Advent season a time of spiritual
preparation.

......................................

# True Praise

*The crowds that went ahead of Him and those that followed shouted, "Hosanna to the Son of David!" "Blessed is He who comes in the name of the Lord!" "Hosanna in the highest!"* (Matthew 21:9)

What a glorious event.
No one deserved the praise more
    than You, Jesus.
As the Messiah, You were worthy of all the
    adoration that came Your way.
Your miracles and acts of compassion had
    captured the imagination of all.
Your message challenged each listener to
    ponder their own relationship with God
    and how they expressed it in their lives.

I wonder how many present
    caught the real message?
How many were there because they were
    attracted by Your personality or because
    they had followed the crowd?
How many were present because it was the
    thing to do?
How many really believed You were the Messiah
    and were willing to follow You to Calvary?

Jesus, I question my own motives for
    worship.
I enjoy the fellowship with other believers.
I get pleasure from listening to the
    music of praise.

I need to hear Your Words
of forgiveness.
I need to participate wholeheartedly
in praising You.
I need to partake of Your Supper.

Guide me as I participate in worship.
Help me consider why I'm here.
Through the power of the Holy Spirit,
enable me to celebrate Your
gift of faith in a meaningful and
sincere way. Amen.

# Waiting for the End

*Therefore keep watch, because you do not know on what day your Lord will come. (Matthew 24:42)*

An article in a news magazine
    predicted the time of Your return,
    Lord.
Does the writer have access to the
    same Bible I do?
Your message is clear, "No one knows about
    that day or hour."

I think about Your return sometimes.
Your return means an end to earthly suffering,
    so I'm ready.
Your return means no more hectic schedules
    and earthly hassles, so I'm eager.
Your return means an end to the bickering that
    plagues earthly relationships,
    so let it happen soon.

Until Your coming, keep me going, Jesus.
Focus my efforts so that I can
    serve You until Your return.
Send Your Spirit to empower me to
    use all the gifts and talents
      You have given me.

Jesus, all time is Your time.
Help me use it creatively and to
    Your glory rather than
      thinking about when it all will end. Amen.

........................................

# Advent

The word *advent* means coming,
   but I want to add "and going" to
   that definition.
That's where I feel I'm meeting myself.
Advent is a busy season with so much
   added pressure during an already
   busy December.
At work there's the challenge to get things done
   before the end of the year.
At home there's the strain of extra activities—
   attending the kids' programs,
   extra choir rehearsals,
   parties and family get-togethers.
And I haven't even thought about shopping.

You sent Your Son into the world as
   the answer, Father.
"Peace on earth," the angels sang.
I plead for peace and quiet.
Lord, slow me down.
In the middle of this hectic schedule,
   help me find time to ponder
   the reason for Christ's birth.
In the middle of all the activity,
   draw me closer to You and
   instill in me a greater appreciation for
   the gift of Your Son.
Come into my life, Lord, and
   prepare my heart for His coming.
Be at the center of all I do during
   the comings and goings of Advent. Amen.

# Week 49 Activities

**Themes:** Advent, Jesus' second coming, peace, praise, preparation, worship

**Old Testament Exploration:** Genesis 3:1–15; Isaiah 9:1–7

**New Testament Exploration:** Matthew 24:36–51; Revelation 22:1–6

> Advent. The coming of quiet joy. Arrival of radiant light in our darkness.
>
> *Anon.*

> The primitive church thought more about the Second Coming of Jesus Christ than about death or about heaven. The early Christians were looking not for a cleft in the ground called a grave but for a cleavage in the sky called Glory. They were watching not for the undertaker but for the uppertaker.
>
> *Alexander Maclaren*

## Reflect

How does God's Holy Spirit lead you to give Him true praise? List 10 things you do to prepare for Christmas. How does God prepare you for Jesus' second coming? Ask God to use this Advent season to prepare your heart and mind for the coming of His Son, Jesus, the Messiah.

# WEEK 50

Brilliant white. Pure. Crystals that catch the winter light and reflect rainbows. What a perfect metaphor for God's cleansing work in your life. He covers the dead landscape of your soul with His pure white forgiveness, won for you by Jesus' death. And you reflect God's saving work when you forgive others and celebrate your faith. Thank God for making you "whiter than snow."

·····································

# Snow

I had forgotten the beauty of
   fresh-fallen snow.
Living in the South, I didn't remember the
   enchantment of Your world
   covered in a layer of white.
My memories were more of cold mornings and
   encounters with a crotchety snow blower.
But now I see the beauty in Your creation again.

The freshness of this day grabs me.
The sun reflects off the snow with a
   dazzling, almost blinding, effect.
The cold air penetrates my lungs and
   issues a wake-up call to my senses.
I'm instantly more alert.

How amazing that a layer of white can
   change my attitude.
I was dark and depressed yesterday,
   just like the weather.
Today I have a fresh, new perspective,
   bright and contagious.
I see Your presence too, Jesus.
The snowy veil is a symbol of Your
   grace and mercy.
The sacrifice of Your blood has made me
   whiter than snow.
I ask for Your Spirit to fill me.
I want to shine with the same intense
   brightness and refresh the lives of
   those around me. Amen.

# Winter

This winter seems especially severe.
Maybe it's my age, but I find
    winter weather increasingly difficult
    to deal with.
But then I awoke this morning to find a
    layer of white covering everything.
Not a heavy snow, just enough to
    cover winter's bleakness.
A freshness pervades the morning.
With my first steps outside,
    my lungs were revived,
    I felt awake and ready to go.

Lord, You knew I needed a fresh start,
    and You gave me a blanket of white.
You reminded me of the special way
    You have made me pure,
    forgiven my sins.
I look at the frozen ground and
    envision the life that lies beneath it.
I think of the potential You have
    placed within me.

Lord, I'm ready to face this day and the
    weeks of winter that remain.
I know that spring and summer will come.
I also know that there are better, more
    pleasant, days ahead for me.
My sins are forgiven. I am Your child.
Thanks for the snow and for touching my life
    in such a special way. Amen.

# Children

*Jesus said, "Let the little children come to Me, and do not hinder them, for the kingdom of heaven belongs to such as these." (Matthew 19:14)*

It's come up once again.
The worship committee at church is
    discussing the problem of
    children in church.
Some people feel their worship is being
    disturbed.
Now they're talking about monitoring the
    noise level and designating the places
    children can sit.

Jesus, that's not Your intention.
Your command is clear, "Let the
    children come to Me."
Your intent is as clear as Your love.
Within Your kingdom there is room for all ...
    and children are especially welcome.

I can identify with those who cherish
    silence.
I reflect on our home and the precious
    time I have for peace and solitude.
I love my children, but I must admit there are
    times I like them more when they're sleeping.

But it can't be that way within the church.
Worship, especially, is for all believers.
Keep me mindful of that, but create an
    awareness among our church leaders and

those who plan our worship.
Empower me as I strive to help my children
   comprehend the wonder of worship.
May our congregation be a community where
   all believers celebrate Your presence and
   experience Your forgiveness. Amen.

........................................

# Week 50 Activities

**Themes:** Children, contentment, joy, nature, renewal, welcome

**Old Testament Exploration:** Psalm 51:7–12; Isaiah 25:1–8

**New Testament Exploration:** Matthew 19:13–14; Luke 1:39–55

> Joy is peace dancing and peace is joy at rest.
>
> *F. B. Meyer*

> Joy is the most infallible sign of the presence of God.
>
> *Léon Henri Marie Bloy*

> We know how God would act if he were in our place—he has been in our place.
>
> *A. W. Tozer*

## Reflect

Do any past sins keep you from enjoying the completeness of God's forgiveness? Confess them now. Read Psalm 51. Ask God to fully restore your joy in your salvation.

## W E E K   5 1

God keeps His promises. Christmas proves that what God says *will* occur. As you sit in church this Christmas, reflect on God's promises for your life. How has He kept them? How is He at work to keep those He hasn't yet fulfilled? Ask God to strengthen your trust in Him. As He opens your eyes to the ways He works, you'll see new reasons to celebrate Christmas every day.

..........................................

# Plotting against Jesus

*An angel of the Lord appeared to Joseph in a dream.*
*"Get up," he said, "take the child and His mother and*
*escape to Egypt. Stay there until I tell you, for Herod*
*is going to search for the child to kill Him." (Matthew*
*2:13)*

How could Herod?
Jesus, You were such a loving man.
You came as the Messiah, to save the
    world.
Your message was love and forgiveness.
King Herod responded to You in fear,
    fear for his earthly throne and power.
        Herod didn't realize that You didn't come
        for his kingdom.
He wanted to remain in control, not
    bend his knee
    to a greater power, his Lord and Savior.
So Herod lost control, and innocent blood
    was spilled.
How could he?

Then I think of the times I've conspired
    against You, Jesus.
My plotting may not be as apparent, but the
    results are just as detrimental.
My schemes usually involve rationalization.
I often spend more time thinking of ways to
    avoid my Christian obligations than
    acting upon them.
I find myself looking for the path of least

resistance instead of taking a walk of
discipleship.

Jesus, forgive me.
Help me see that Herod's actions were
part of the plan, part of the
path You traveled from the
manger hay of Bethlehem
to the open grave of Easter morning.
That was Your Father's plan.
Now through the power of the Holy Spirit,
enable me to plan new ways to serve You
rather than ways to avoid sharing Your
message. Amen.

# Christmas

This is Your day, Father.
Easter belongs to Jesus and
 His victory over death,
 but Christmas belongs to You.
I can't imagine the struggle You must have
 gone through.
You allowed Your Son to become a
 human being and not only face
 the humiliation of a human life
 but even death itself.
And Jesus did it for the sake of all people,
 many of whom couldn't care less.

Sometimes this fact restrains my Christmas
 celebration.
All the world appears joyful as
 "Peace on earth" becomes the cliché
 of the day.
Everyone becomes religious as they
 celebrate the birth of a Child
 they might not know personally.
Father, others might struggle to understand
 my melancholy attitude.
But as a father, I reflect on Your cost.
I pray that You would make me a disciple
 worthy of the price You and Jesus paid.
As a sinner, I know I can never measure up.
And as a redeemed saint, I know I can never
 stop trying.
Father, thanks for Christmas and the new life
 You have given me. Amen.

........................................

# The Day after Christmas

The mixed feelings that go with
    this day always astound me.
I can sense it in those around me.
The peace and joy of Christmas have been
    replaced by a combination of relief
    and exhaustion.
The world returns to normal as people
    dismantle the decorations and
    return unwanted gifts.

Lord, it's not supposed to be this way.
The gift of the Savior is a gift for all days.
When we quickly move past the celebration,
    we belittle Your benevolence.

Father, as a member of Your family,
    make the celebration of
    my Savior's birth a time of
    personal spiritual renewal and
    rededication.
Motivate me every day in my
    service to You with Your
    sacrificial love as shown in the
    gift of Your Son.

Make the joy of Christmas an
    eternal presence in my life.
I want the sights and sounds of Christmas to
    dwell in my heart all year.
Make me a witness both to the
    joy of Christmas and the
    new life that is mine because of Jesus. Amen.

# Week 51 Activities

**Theme:** Jesus

**Old Testament Exploration:** Ruth 4:13–22; Isaiah 11:1–16

**New Testament Exploration:** Luke 2:1–20; John 1:1–18

> Ah, dearest Jesus, holy Child,
> Make Thee a bed, soft, undefiled,
> Within my heart, that it may be
> A quiet chamber kept for Thee.
>
> *Martin Luther*

> Once in the year and only once, the whole world stands still to celebrate the advent of a life. Only Jesus claims this worldwide, undying remembrance.
>
> *Anon.*

> Filling the world he lies in a manger.
>
> *St. Augustine*

> Jesus' coming is the final and unanswerable proof that God cares.
>
> *William Barclay*

## Reflect

How do you celebrate the Savior's birth? What traditions have you brought from your childhood into your adult life? How does God work through your Christmas activities to remind you of His great love? Memorize Luther's Christmas prayer. Teach it to your family and say it before bed on Christmas Eve.

Praise to the Lord!
Oh, let all that is in me adore Him!
All that has life and breath, come now with
     praises before Him!
Let the amen
Sound from His people again.
Gladly forever adore Him!

# In Search of Contentment

*But godliness with contentment is great gain.* (*1 Timothy 6:6*)

You are the provider of
   all things, Father.
I am constantly reminded of Your
   promise to care for me.
And I must admit that I have more than what
   my life requires.
But I struggle with contentment.

I fight the battle on two grounds.
First, I'm not satisfied with what I have.
I fall victim to our materialistic
   culture.
I want even more despite having
   more than I need.

Secondly, I struggle to find happiness
   in my life.
I'm constantly restless.
I'm not happy with my job.
I feel no sense of satisfaction.
I long for new challenges instead of
   completing what I've started.

The answer lies in You.
Guide me so that my satisfaction
   is found in a stronger, growing
   relationship with You.

Lord, help me find contentment in the
   gift of Your Son.
Knowing that I am a redeemed child of God
   should always be sufficient. Amen.

# New Year's Eve

This year has been a gift from You, Lord.
While not everything has gone as I would
  have liked, I have experienced
  Your grace and forgiveness each day.
I have been more aware of Your presence.

I pause today to celebrate and say thanks.
While others might be preparing to
  cheer the beginning of a new year
  with parties and revelry,
I quietly reflect. Your goodness amazes me.

Midnight might be the beginning of a
  new year, but as one of Your
  baptized children, it will mark
  another new day.
I don't need to wait to make resolutions.
Each day offers the opportunity to
  begin again.
Each day gives me a reason to
  celebrate Your goodness.
Father, it's such a blessing to be part of
  Your kingdom. Amen.

# Alleluia

It's such a simple word, *alleluia.*
I've said it thousands of times in worship.
I've even shouted it at home,
like the time Katie struggled with a
difficult math concept.
When she finally got it, it seemed
like the thing to say.

You are so good to me, Lord.
You are so loving.
There has to be a special way to say it.
And You have given us the word—
*Alleluia!*—Praise the Lord!

But *alleluia* needs to be more than just
a word.
It needs to be a way of life.
My life lived for You, in realization of
all that You do for me, needs to
shout *alleluia* in all I do and say.

Lord, help me live my *alleluias.*
May others see Your love in me.
Help me face each day,
each opportunity to shout *alleluia,*
as Your forgiven child.
Father, help my life to be one tremendous
**ALLELUIA!** Amen.

# Week 52 Activities

**Themes:** Contentment, new beginnings, praise, thanksgiving, time

**Old Testament Exploration:** Psalm 103

**New Testament Exploration:** Revelation 22:12–21

> I suppose when we wake on January 1 the world will look the same. But there is a reminder of the Resurrection at the start of each new year, each new decade. That's why I also like sunrises, Mondays, and new seasons. God seems to be saying, "With me you can always start afresh."
>
> *Ada Lum*

## Reflect

As you look back over the last year, how has God been present and active in your life? How has He strengthened you? How has He caused you to grow? How has He stilled your fears and brought you peace?

..........................................

> "Peace I leave with you; My peace I give you. I do not give to you as the world gives. Do not let your hearts be troubled and do not be afraid."
>
> *Jesus Christ* (John 14:27)